Scorpio

24 October – 22 November

First published in Great Britain 2009
by Harlequin Mills & Boon Limited,
Eton House, 18-24 Paradise Road, Richmond, Surrey TW9 1SR

Copyright © Dadhichi Toth 2008 & 2009

ISBN: 978 0 263 87072 5

Typeset at Midland Typesetters Australia

Harlequin Mills & Boon policy is to use papers that are natural, renewable and recyclable products and made from wood grown in sustainable forests. The logging and manufacturing processes conform to the legal environmental regulations of the country of origin.

Printed and bound in Spain
by Litografia Rosés S.A., Barcelona

About
Dadhichi

Dadhichi is one of Australia's foremost astrologers. He has the ability to draw from complex astrological theory to provide clear, easily understandable advice and insights for people who want to know what their future might hold.

In the 26 years that Dadhichi has been practising astrology, face reading and other esoteric studies, he has conducted over 9,500 consultations. His clients include celebrities, political and diplomatic figures, and media and corporate identities from all over the world.

Dadhichi's unique blend of astrology and face reading helps people fulfil their true potential. His extensive experience practising western astrology is complemented by his research into the theory and practice of eastern systems of astrology.

Dadhichi features in numerous newspapers and magazines and he also appears regularly on many of Australia's leading television and radio networks, where many of his political and worldwide forecasts have proved uncannily accurate.

His website www.astrology.com.au is now one of the top ten online Australian lifestyle sites and, in conjunction with www.facereader.com, www.soulconnector.com and www.psychjuice.com, they attract over half a million visitors monthly. The websites offer a wide variety of features, helpful information and personal services.

Dedicated to The Light of Intuition
Sri V. Krishnaswamy—mentor and friend
With thanks to Julie, Joram, Isaac and Janelle

Welcome from
Dadhichi

Dear Friend,

Welcome! It's great to have you here, reading your horoscope, trying to learn more about yourself and what's in store for you in 2010.

I visited Mexico a while ago and stumbled upon the Mayan prophecies for 2012, which, they say, is the year when the longstanding calendar we use in the western world supposedly stops! If taken literally, some people could indeed believe that 'the end of the world is near'. However, I see it differently.

Yes, it might seem as though the world is getting harder and harder to deal with, especially when fear enters our lives. But, I believe that 'the end' indicated by these Mayan prophecies has more to do with the end that will create new beginnings for our societies, more to do with making changes to our material view of life and some necessary adjustments for the human race to progress and prosper in future. So let's get one thing straight: you and I will both be around after 2012, reading our 2013 horoscopes!

My prediction and advice centres around keeping a cool mind and not reacting to the fear that could overtake us. Of course, this isn't easy, especially when media messages might increase our anxiety about such things as the impacts of global warming or the scarcity of fossil fuels.

I want you to understand that it is certainly important to be aware and play your part in making the world a better place; however, the best and surest way to support global goals is to help yourself first. Let me explain. If everyone focused just a little more on improving *themselves* rather than just pointing their finger to criticise others, it would result in a dramatic change and improvement; not just globally, but societally. And, of course, you mustn't forget what a positive impact this would have on your personal relationships as well.

Astrology focuses on self-awareness; your own insights into your personality, thinking processes and relationships. This is why this small book you have in your hand doesn't only concentrate on what is going to happen, but more importantly how you can *make* things happen positively through being your best.

I have always said that there are two types of people: puppets and actors. The first simply react to each outside stimulus and are therefore slaves of their environment, and even of their own minds and emotions. They are puppets in the hands of karma. The other group I call actors. Although they can't control what happens to them all the time, either, they are better able to adapt and gain something purposeful in their lives. They are in no way victims of circumstance.

I hope you will use what is said in the following pages to become the master of your destiny, and not rely on the predictions that are given as mere fate but as valuable guidelines to use intelligently when life presents you with its certain challenges.

Neither the outside world, nor the ups and downs that occur in your life, should affect your innermost spirituality and self-confidence. Take control: look beyond your current challenges and use them as the building blocks of experience to create success and fulfilment in the coming year.

I believe you have the power to become great and shine your light for all to see. I hope your 2010 horoscope book will be a helpful guide and inspiration for you.

Warm regards, and may the stars shine brightly for you in 2010!

Your Astrologer

Dadhichi Toth

Contents

The Scorpio
Identity

Perfection is achieved, not when there is nothing left to add, but when there is nothing left to take away.

—Antoine de St Exupery

Scorpio: A Snapshot

Key Characteristics

Secretive, passionate, determined, tactless, loyal, hardworking and inflexible

Compatible Star Signs

Scorpio, Taurus, Capricorn, Cancer, Pisces

Key Life Phrase

I will

Life Goals

To transform yourself into the best you can become

Platinum Assets

Ability to overcome at all costs, sexual attractiveness and willpower

Zodiac Totems

The scorpion, the lizard, the phoenix

Zodiac Symbol

♍

Zodiac Facts

Eighth sign of the zodiac; fixed, fertile, feminine, moist

Element

Water

Famous Scorpios

Joaquin Phoenix, Winona Ryder, Bill Gates,
Henry Winkler, Larry Flynt, Joni Mitchell,
David Schwimmer, Ethan Hawke, Demi Moore,
Leonardo Di Caprio, Whoopi Goldberg,
Chris Noth, Danny De Vito, Owen Wilson, Calvin Klein,
Jodie Foster, Larry King, Bjork, Pablo Picasso

Scorpio: Your profile

It doesn't bother you in the least that people regard you as a 'hard nut to crack'. No doubt, being born under the sign of Scorpio, you are the most complex of individuals. But you wouldn't change it for a thing, would you? You're proud of the fact that you're a Scorpion and use this to your advantage in most of life's situations.

The water sign of Scorpio is also of a fixed nature, meaning that, like ice, you can be called aloof and often very difficult to understand. However, you more than make up for this with your intuitive and curious mind.

You have an incredible power of insight, which you use socially, professionally and ultimately spiritually to obtain the higher gifts of nature. This is one of the more important elements of your personality that attracts others. But over and above this mystical, mysterious side to your personality, you are passionate and also ooze loads of sexual appeal and personal magnetism.

You're an exciting person to be with, not just because of your immense appeal but because you have an innate curiosity about people, about life, and want to know everything about everyone. This is why you're also well suited to the occult and mystical fields of endeavour such as palm reading, astrology and generally any sort of psychic science.

You are committed to understanding relationships, and there are no half measures for you. So as well as demanding a lot from yourself, you expect just as much from others. Fortunately you realise not everyone is able to reach the standards you set.

You are determined in life, forceful, and have high ambitions. In fact, you like to put yourself in the fire and expect yourself to be better than everyone else. You believe that in life only a select few can achieve the pinnacle of success and, irrespective of what you choose on your path and however long it takes, as a Scorpio you are sure to be successful in the end.

You are quite obstinate in your opinions and people sometimes find you a little overbearing. You push yourself and everyone else's belief systems to the limit. Actually, there are times when you like to test people to see just how much they know and also how much they can handle. You are loyal and expect loyalty in return.

You are able to bewitch people. It's not easy to put your finger on this power, but there's something mesmerising and persuasive, not just about your words, but about your very presence. It's impossible to miss or overlook a Scorpio if they happen to walk into a room. You generate a specific sort of energy that is arresting, all consuming and very enticing. For this reason, people will always be mysteriously drawn to you. How you handle this will be your double-edged sword and major lesson in life, particularly regarding your relationships and sexuality.

Compulsion, intensity and a passionate drive for anything you set your mind and heart upon are the likely verses behind your personality. When it comes to the lower aspects of life, you need to be on guard because you can spiral into a compulsive, obsessive fascination with the dark side.

Actually, many Scorpios gain a deep understanding of life through exploring the darker, more mysterious aspects of sexuality and other hedonistic practices. This is okay as long as you maintain control and do it purely as an experiment to rid yourself of your limiting personality traits.

With such a strong character, you tend to hate weakness in any form. You see this as something that must be eliminated. You can eliminate it so well from your own self, but be careful: not everyone has the same strength or is at the same stage of evolution as you, which could make you appear much more ruthless than you really are.

You can be vengeful and sarcastic if someone crosses you or displays any form of disloyalty. Your expectations are so high of them that you sometimes forget we are, after all, only human. It's all or nothing for you, Scorpio, which can be a great source of strength and success but also your downfall as well, particularly in relationships.

Scorpios believe that they have been born to win. You certainly are a winner but can also be overly competitive and this is fine as long as you don't alienate others through the sheer force of your personality. Try to relax a little and give others a chance to express themselves as well.

If you were born between the 24th of October and the 2nd of November you possess the typical Scorpio intensity. You're also sensual as well, possessing noble and spiritual aspirations along with that. Handling pressure will initially be part of your challenge before you eventually become more spiritual later in life.

If you're a Scorpion born between the 3rd and the 11th of November, you're idealistic and also extremely spiritual by birth. You want to understand people, yourself and, for the most part, life in general so you'll be constantly enquiring into the philosophical reasons for why things are the way they are.

If you were born between the 12th and the 22nd of November, you are sensitive to a fault. This is because the Moon and the sign of Cancer also have some sway over your personality and your birth.

Your main challenge in life is to develop more self-control and not be overwhelmed by what happens to you in life.

Scorpio role model: Bill Gates

Scorpios are known for their sheer determination and ambition. This is perfectly seen in the multi-billionaire Bill Gates. Bill worked long and hard pursuing his own path to make a name for himself through his Microsoft Corporation. Like him, you too have a unique destiny and can succeed on your own terms.

Scorpio: The light side

You're a great lover, as shown by Scorpio ruling the eighth sexual zone of the zodiac. You understand love, the mystery of attraction and the power of persuasion over romantic partners. You love wholeheartedly and make this almost a religious experience, but you also need someone who can love you with the same depth and intensity.

Transformation is your second name. In anything you do, you like to stamp it with the Scorpio emblem of passion, ingenuity and success. There are no half measures in your life, and you work with focus and intensity; not so much for the results but for the experience of being in the moment and doing great work.

Silence is also one of your greatest attributes and you use it with great skill. Yet, you are a master wordsmith. When the occasion requires it, you can use language to achieve anything you so desire.

One of the lesser known powers of Scorpio is your ability to heal. You have wonderful hands and your mere presence is capable of making people feel good. You are also very intuitive, having a sixth sense.

Scorpio: The shadow side

Some Scorpios manipulate others to their own advantage. You must be careful not to use your psychic or intellectual powers to overcome those who are weaker than you. This can be a major test for you in life. However, as long as you're aware of it you'll be able to upturn your strengths so they are used for the better good.

Some of the darker traits of Scorpio include compulsion, obsession, resentment and possessiveness, especially in matters of sensuality and sexuality. Bring these aspects of your character under control by focusing on creative and artistic activities. By redirecting these energies, you will create something of worth that doesn't undermine you or destroy your relationships.

Scorpios become resentful and carry their emotional baggage around for years. If you don't let go, this can cause disease in time. Simply let go.

You push yourself to the limits, to test just how much your body and mind can handle. Some say this is your ego trying to impress others, but that's not quite the truth. You love to challenge yourself, but in doing so may also end up ruining your relationships by focusing solely on one thing to the exclusion of others. Lead a balanced life.

Scorpio woman

When you meet a Scorpio woman for the first time, you might tend to have mixed reactions towards her. Of course, you'll find her seductive, feminine and alluring, but there's a harder edge to her as well, which could scare you! Hers is not the average day-to-day femininity found in others.

This is a progressive new age woman who takes what she wants and doesn't accept anything less than what her ideals demand. If you're a Scorpio woman reading this, you know exactly what I'm talking about. Yes, you are magnetically attractive but also deadly at the same time, just like your totem, the scorpion.

Perhaps the Scorpio woman could better be described as a black widow spider than a scorpion? You do have a tendency to despise any sort of weakness and, if you find over time that a business partner, a lover or even a friend exhibits weakness of any sort, you will destroy them if you can't transform them first!

Your deepest desire is to help others, to transform them and show them the way. Although, you do have the tendency to be a little overbearing in the way you present your ideas. On many occasions you feel as though you are right and everyone else is wrong. It's a case of 'your way or the highway'. The middle path can be difficult for you because Scorpio women are usually quite inflexible in their ways.

Scorpio women, especially those born in the early part of Scorpio, can idealise love and make excessive demands on their partners. You could sometimes blame others for not being able to meet the set requirements and prerequisites of what you regard as essential for a successful relationship. But think again. If you are pushing, prodding and demanding in your Scorpionic manner, it could be you that is the cause of failure in some of your relationships.

Be softer; allow that feminine, emotional aspect of your character to shine through. Use your charm and magnetic prowess to do the job rather than your vehement, poisonous tongue, of which you are fully aware because it often acts before your brain kicks in! Think first, then speak; or better still, use that uncanny power of silence that is your trademark.

The Scorpio woman is a super woman! You have an immense amount of confidence, being able to juggle executive or business life with the family and marital and social commitments. And you do everything super well. The only problem here is that you could become a workaholic and forget number one; that is, yourself.

Sexually you are a dynamic powerhouse and need a partner who can fulfil these needs. You are 100 per cent intensely committed to your relationships and need a mate who can also reciprocate in the same measure.

No one can twist you around their little finger and you are an impeccable judge of character due to the extraordinary level of intuition you possess. This seems to be an inbuilt trait of the Scorpion-born individual, particularly women. You know within 30 seconds whether or not a person is honest or worthwhile just by looking at them. You probably don't even know how you do this but you can usually trust your intuition to give you the correct answers.

Because you are so committed to your ideals, you are somewhat outspoken in your opinions. You never hold back and tell others exactly how you feel. You must therefore be prepared to make a few enemies along the way. But as long as you're true to yourself, this is not going to be of too much concern to the genuinely Scorpio woman.

Scorpio man

Don't be mistaken when I use the word 'passionate' to summarise the Scorpio male. Sure, sex does play a significant part in his life, but we need to use the broader sense of the word to mean a passion for life, an intensity of purpose, which is exactly how we can best describe a man born under the sign of Scorpio.

You are intense and determined about life and what you do, and it's rare to find a Scorpio doing something that doesn't resonate with his spirit. Being a Scorpio man, you want to live an exciting and dynamic life, one in which you can express your inner self and perfect your craft, whatever that might be.

You consider yourself the master of your fate and will live life only on your terms, even if that involves a tremendous amount of sacrifice. Some Scorpio men come from poor or very hard backgrounds. It's this training ground in life that makes them ready to forebear some of the most difficult circumstances, which ultimately make them stronger, more resilient human beings who achieve such success that others wonder how it is possible.

The Scorpio male is very, very secretive and doesn't like others to know much about him, even though they themselves are constantly investigating and prying into other people's minds to gain the upper hand. The irony is, if they feel for even just one moment that someone else is getting a handle on who they are and what their motivations may be, they'll probably run away and disappear. Such is the mystery of the Scorpio male, who wants to remain an enigma.

As a Scorpio male, you understand full well your ability to hypnotise with your magnetic eyes any prospective mate that comes within an orbit of a couple of metres. It's like the rabbit being bedazzled by the headlights of an oncoming car and being hit before it even knew what was coming. Your power, your passion and love are all very real, and only a rare few can withstand your energy.

You have a marvellous capacity for exploring the depths of not only sexuality but the psychology of relationships as well. Scorpios are natural-born psychotherapists, so beware: the newly met Scorpio male can 'undress' a person's mind, too, not just their body!

You should never try to hide anything from a Scorpio male. Men born under this sign are inbuilt investigators, detectives of the highest order, even though they may not have trained at a police academy. You may not even realise they are questioning you but all the while they are piecing together the bits of information that will give them the ammunition they need to ambush you, without any mercy.

If you cross a Scorpio, rest assured you will feel their vengeance. It may not be immediate but Scorpios are capable of biding their time until they can conclude their 'business'. This may take years but the task will be accomplished. In short, the Scorpio male is vengeful but also loving and forgiving if you quickly concede your errors.

Scorpio child

Scorpio children may sometimes appear to be brooding, introverted and antisocial. However, this is only because they experience such a refined and sensitive mental development that they want to understand the world and its people. They are curious creatures who are constantly investigating the ins and outs of anything they happen to find.

The young Scorpio child has intense feelings and they need lots of love to help them develop their personality. You need to give them time, care and help nurture their strong intuitive sense. If you're constantly finding yourself too busy and unable to share time with them, rest assured they won't forget this and years later you'll pay for such a mistake.

The Scorpio child has a wilful mind and is determined, knowing exactly what he or she wants. Don't try to sway them, because it won't work. They are the consummate salespeople of the zodiac and can wear you down by persistently demanding what they want until you give in.

Scorpio is a fixed and brittle sign, and its children can be resilient and able to shoulder huge responsibilities at an early age. In fact, they feel destined to do that from the moment they can walk. They challenge themselves as well as others. They are excellent competitors and so sports will be an avenue in which they can vent their Scorpionic tendencies. They are fair but ruthless players of any sport.

Academically, the Scorpio child can be an excellent student. As long as they enjoy what they're involved with, they will make a commitment to finishing the work and doing it to the best of their ability. But they can also be distracted if the work is 'beneath' them. They need careful direction to keep them challenged enough to stick with it.

Scorpio children explore both their inner and outer worlds. You mustn't speak down to them because they probably have a deeper understanding of life and philosophy that even you do. Talk to them with respect and you'll be amazed at what truths and insights they're able to share back with you.

Scorpio children are quite secretive and you need to respect this. But if you also sense they are troubled and not able to share some of their emotional angst, you'll be challenged in how you can actually draw them out of themselves. This is probably one of the harder aspects of life with your Scorpio child.

Romance, love and marriage

We've already spoken considerably and at length about the irresistible personal energy that you, as a Scorpio, exude. Your emotions run much deeper than anyone else's, perhaps more than even you understand. Therefore, before embarking on any sort of relationship with anyone, the most important foundation you need is self-understanding. You must never shy away from this because if you don't understand yourself, as complex as you are, how is anyone else going to understand this most fascinating and complex sign of the zodiac called Scorpio?

As a Scorpio, relationships are extraordinarily important to you but then again so is your personal and private space. Balancing these two parts of your life could be difficult, so you need someone who is particularly sensitive and who can react in just the right sort of way to give you the space you need when you need it, but to also give you the sexual and emotional intensity that you yearn for as well.

Unless your partner is sufficiently evolved, they may not understand that your silence, your looks and gestures, are your way of acknowledging them and also of showing your love, probably in a more profound way than touching, kissing or gifts. The less sensitive individual might dismiss you as being cold, aloof and insensitive to them, but this is not really you. Perhaps at least in the first stages of your relationship, coming to know this could be a subtle test for them. After all, you do believe you deserve the best, and you'll want to weed out some of the less than desirable individuals, won't you?

You need someone who's happy to join you in the roller-coaster ride of life, someone with strength, adventure and even the desire to get into a tempestuous lifestyle with you. You want someone who's happy to take on the challenge of being in love with an intense and complex Scorpio, right?

Once you set your eye upon someone you consider a worthy lover, you don't let go. If you're still in the initial stages of the chase, you'll do what it takes to woo that person and to keep them. Once you've won their heart, however, you must relax a little because you do have the tendency to regard your lover or spouse as a possession. This is a mistake. By smothering your other half you only cause them to pull back and withhold the love you probably deserve. You give 150 per cent to the person you love and, unfortunately, not everyone is able to reciprocate with the same level of intensity as someone like yourself born under Scorpio.

In love you must learn to control your deep emotions and moodiness. Many Scorpios tend to be swayed by these shifting moods, which can create a great barrier to further satisfaction in love and marriage. When you shut down, withdraw and choose not to interact, you become so distant that you're completely out of reach, out of touch. Often you use your silence as a form of punishment; but if you're honest with yourself, you'll realise that this only punishes you as well because then you don't have the benefit of the love and interaction you so desperately desire. You must try at all costs to overcome these limitations of your Scorpionic personality so that your communication and general destiny romantically will be pure and fulfilling.

You'll fare well with the water and earth signs of the zodiac; that is, Cancer, Pisces, Virgo and Capricorn. These individuals understand you and some of your moods better than others. The opposite star sign to Scorpio is Taurus, who can act as a countermeasure to some of the more emotional and destructive aspects of your personality.

Finally, both men and women born under Scorpio are excellent home-makers who love family life and children. You have a natural inclination towards love, family life and supporting the ones you've taken under your wing with everything you have.

By balancing the negative traits of possessiveness, jealousy and moodiness, you can enjoy a tremendously fulfilling romantic and passionate life.

Health, wellbeing and diet

Your emotions are probably one of the main causes of your poor health, particularly if you're a Scorpio who tends to hold onto grudges, withhold feelings, and let your moodiness run rampant. Many health issues are caused by your inability to overcome these simple internal emotional energies.

The reproductive areas, kidneys and the excretory system are the prime constitutional areas ruled by the sign you were born under. You must keep these parts of your body clean and in good condition through drinking water and also avoiding intoxicants and other spicy foods.

If you're like most Scorpios, you have a reasonably long working day and your search for perfection may cause you to become a workaholic. Sleep is absolutely essential even though you may feel as though you don't need it. Get your seven or eight hours a night and you'll notice the difference.

Because you hold in a lot of feelings and are emotionally intense, physical sport is a great way for you to balance this component of your life as well. You have strong competitive urges, and these coupled with an immense willpower means you can not only let off steam but also be successful through some of your sporting engagements.

The water signs including Scorpio do have a tendency to use food as a means of coping emotionally. Don't let food be a comfort but rather eat for health and vitality. Try eating smaller meals and don't drink too much when you're eating because this may reduce your capacity to digest and absorb some of the nutrients.

Spicy foods, chilli and other exotic dishes rich and high in calories may appeal to you due to the rulership of your star sign by Mars and Pluto. These foods can be irritating to your stomach lining and also highly exciting to your personality. Eating them could adversely affect not only your physical wellbeing but your psychological wellbeing as well. Moderate the use of spices in your diet.

Pumpkin, beetroot, sweet potato and any of the other orange and red vegetables are great resources of nutrition for those born under Scorpio. You also need a sufficient intake of protein to cope with the excessive demands you make on your physical being. Red beans, lentils and other high protein sources from vegetable products, if you are a vegetarian, are excellent to help you with this. If you're a meat eater, lean white meat or fish can also provide you with the additional energy you require. Again, eat smaller meals, and you should never eat when you're emotionally upset or under stress.

Work

Those born under Scorpio enjoy any manner of professional activities because their minds are versatile and adaptable. You have the ability to work in any sort of investigative or medical field with great results. Many great surgeons, psychologists and psychiatrists are born under Scorpio because they have that natural inclination to understand and to heal.

Metaphysical or psychic healing can also be areas that attract many Scorpios. Your intuitive power and healing energy are things you can foster naturally, even if you don't want to pursue them in a career per se.

Criminology comes under the jurisdiction of Scorpio. Police work, investigation, forensic medical activities and anything that is hidden such as metals, gold mining, petroleum and other geological resources fall under suitable work for Scorpio.

Jupiter's influence over your finance sector gives you a taste for earning money and, even if you're not interested in such areas early in your life, later you will naturally gravitate towards achieving success financially.

Scorpio is a successful sign and indicates money, fame and a great deal of satisfaction in the future for you, particularly if you choose a career that is in keeping with something you love doing.

Key to karma, spirituality and emotional balance

The key words for Scorpio are 'I will'. There's nothing much in life you can't achieve, but increasing and maintaining control could be one of the major challenges for you spiritually. You must learn to be flexible and accept that you are not able to control everything that happens in life.

The idea of surrender is an important one for you and can help you develop your spiritual insights so that you can become unconditional in both your work and your personal relationships. Try not to challenge everyone on points of difference but look at the similarities instead. This will foster peace in your life.

You can meditate with good results on Mondays, Tuesdays and Sundays, which will bring you a greater degree of peace, tranquillity and connectedness to the universe as a whole.

Your lucky days

Your luckiest days are Mondays, Tuesdays, Thursdays and Sundays.

Your lucky numbers

Remember that the forecasts given later in the book will help you optimise your chances of winning. Your lucky numbers are:

9, 18, 27, 36, 45, 54

3, 12, 21, 30, 48, 57

2, 11, 20, 29, 38, 47, 56

Your destiny years

Your most important years are 9, 18, 27, 36, 45, 54, 63, 72 and 81.

SCORPIO

Star Sign
Compatibility

By all means marry; if you get a good wife,
you'll be happy. If you get a bad one,
you'll become a philosopher.

—Socrates

Romantic compatibility

How compatible are you with your current partner, lover or friend? Did you know that astrology can reveal a whole new level of understanding between people simply by looking at their star sign and that of their partner? In this chapter I'd like to share some special insights that will help you better appreciate your strengths and challenges using Sun sign compatibility.

The Sun reflects your drive, willpower and personality. The essential qualities of two star signs blend like two pure colours, producing an entirely new colour. Relationships, similarly, produce their own emotional colours when two people interact. The following is a general guide to your romantic prospects with others and how, by knowing the astrological 'colour' of each other, the art of love can help you create a masterpiece.

When reading the following I ask you to remember that no two star signs are ever *totally* incompatible. With effort and compromise, even the most 'difficult' astrological matches can work. Don't close your mind to the full range of life's possibilities! Learning about each other and ourselves is the most important facet of astrology.

Quick-reference guide: Horoscope compatibility between signs (percentage)

	Aries	Taurus	Gemini	Cancer	Leo	Virgo	Libra	Scorpio	Sagittarius	Capricorn	Aquarius	Pisces
Pisces	65	85	50	90	75	70	50	95	75	85	55	80
Aquarius	55	80	90	70	70	50	95	60	60	70	80	55
Capricorn	50	95	50	45	45	95	85	65	55	85	70	85
Sagittarius	90	50	75	55	95	70	80	80	85	55	60	75
Scorpio	80	85	60	95	75	85	85	90	85	65	60	95
Libra	70	75	90	60	65	80	80	85	80	85	95	50
Virgo	45	90	75	75	75	70	80	85	70	95	50	70
Leo	90	70	80	70	85	75	65	75	95	45	70	75
Cancer	65	80	60	75	70	75	60	95	55	45	70	90
Gemini	65	70	75	60	80	75	90	60	75	50	90	50
Taurus	65	70	70	80	70	90	75	85	50	95	80	85
Aries	60	70	70	65	90	45	70	80	90	50	55	65

Each star sign combination is followed by the elements of those star signs and the result of their combining. For instance, Aries is a fire sign and Aquarius is an air sign and this combination produces a lot of 'hot air'. Air feeds fire and fire warms air. In fact, fire requires air. However, not all air and fire combinations work. I have included information about the different birth periods within each star sign and this will throw even more light on your prospects for a fulfilling love life with any star sign you choose.

Good luck in your search for love, and may the stars shine upon you in 2010!

Compatibility quick-reference guide

Each of the twelve star signs has a greater or lesser affinity with one another. The quick-reference guide will show you who's hot and who's not so hot as far as your relationships are concerned.

SCORPIO + ARIES
Water + Fire = Steam

Love between Scorpio and Aries is passionate but also challenging. Both of you are extremely energetic, expressive of your love, and sexually very intense. On top of this, you are both fiercely independent and it's likely that head-on confrontations will occur from time to time.

Because your personalities are extremely forceful, power plays will be the cornerstone of your relationship. Dealing with such issues will determine whether or not the two of you can last as a couple. Your willpower is as strong as Aries and, as you know, two people usually can't rule the roost at once. Taking the underdog position to each other will be a hard call for both of you.

The Aries' power is unbridled, spontaneous, but certainly very creative, and Scorpios are often attracted to these kinds of people. It can create a compelling friendship if you decide to give it a go. There's an immediate attraction between the two of you, and your sexual powers will entice each other.

Aries enjoys variety in life and usually has many hobbies and outside interests. You, Scorpio, could find yourself feeling a little insecure with their fun-loving revelry, so be careful that it doesn't bring out the more possessive and dominant streak in your nature. Aries is militant and totally independent and likes to control his or her own destiny. They don't want to take a backseat to your overbearing demands and commanding nature.

Generally speaking, the passion factor will keep your relationship alive. However, this is also a relationship that has considerable instability at the heart of it, so making this a long-term, committed partnership is difficult, to say the least.

Intimacy is exciting between you and even though Aries is sometimes a little more superficial than you are in the bedroom, they will still give you plenty of satisfaction between the sheets. Scorpio and Aries equally find sex important, and on this level your similar drives will satisfy these sexual aspects of your character.

If the two of you can be less self-centred and consider the other person's needs a little more, your relationship will improve dramatically.

If you team up with an Aries born between the 21st and the 30th of March, this is a combative relationship that will challenge both of you on every level. It's important not to let mind games dominate the emotional landscape in this relationship. You need to give Aries the space they need to live their lives on their terms and, if that's possible, your sexual relationship will satisfy you and make up for these other shortcomings.

With Aries born between the 31st of March and the 10th of April, you need to deal with their dominant personality and also their professional appetites. If they make these their priorities, it will severely undermine the relationship. Because you don't like being second in command, this could be a terrible combination, so think twice before involving yourself.

Aries born between the 11th and 20th of April are probably the best match for you, Scorpio, because they have the planet Jupiter and Sagittarius strongly influencing their lives. There's a powerful karmic connection between the two of you, and therefore you'll find plenty to occupy you and make you feel close, both mentally and physically.

SCORPIO + TAURUS
Water + Earth = Mud

Many of you born under Scorpio will be attracted to your opposite sign of Taurus. There's an emotional and physical connection that is undeniable. But, having said this, the fact is you're also very different and stubborn in your basic nature. Neither of you will yield and therefore flexibility is the key word for a successful relationship between Scorpio and Taurus.

One of the best pieces of advice I can give you, Scorpio, when relating to Taurus, is that sooner or later you may need to learn how to walk away from discussions, or should I say arguments, that go around in circles. If you're trying to convince Taurus of your opinion, or vice versa, you'll soon realise that neither of you is going to budge. You'll have to concede defeat, even if you know you are right on many occasions. The funny thing is that Taurus will feel exactly the same way.

Taurus is determined, ambitious and also very practical. This reflects many of your own personality traits, which is what, in a strange way, attracts you to them.

Taurus irritates you sometimes because they're just so finicky about the practicality of things. You like to leave a little room for the unknown—the mystical element and what you call 'the X factor'. But Taurus feels so uncomfortable with all that stuff. They are pragmatic individuals who need to touch, feel and see things to believe them. If you're just getting off the ground in a relationship and have ideas for your own life, especially financially, you'll need to deal with this aspect of Taurus's controlling nature. Get used to it. They know best when it comes to money matters and, believe it or not, you'll probably find yourself doing quite well if you stick with them because their commercial instincts are usually correct.

They say Scorpio is deep and silent and also very secretive, but this is just a superficial view of Scorpio. In love, they desperately need to communicate their feelings and for you, Scorpio, this is where Taurus may also at times let you down. They have a tendency to bottle up their feelings, hold onto grudges and not reciprocate in the way you would like them to. You will need to connect with them on a deeper level to understand their deeper needs and what's going on within their hearts.

Generally Scorpio gets on well with Taurus; however, if you team up with someone born between the 21st and the 29th of April, you'll be very satisfied with your choice. This can be a match made in heaven and marriage is certainly not out of the question with them.

There's a strong attraction between you and any Taurean born between the 30th of April and the 10th of May, but this may begin more as a friendship than a deeply committed sexual relationship. There's a strong social flavour about this friendship. Initially, neither of you will feel all that comfortable about taking your friendship any further. Who will make the first move?

Most Taureans are excellent businesspeople and those born between the 11th and the 21st of May are even more so. You have different approaches to money, so discussion is essential before you commit yourselves to each other. If you can understand who owns what and what your material contributions are going to be to this relationship, then your emotional and sexual lives together are likely to fare much better.

SCORPIO + GEMINI
Water + Air = Rain

It will be easy for you to become lured by Gemini's exciting imagination and quick-witted conversation. But don't act too quickly because there's much more to love than idle chit-chat, isn't there, Scorpio?

I may as well come right out and say that you and Gemini are one of the least compatible combinations of the zodiac. Therefore, you could be getting yourself into much deeper waters than you could ever imagine. Geminis can leave you high and dry because they are very fickle, sometimes superficial, and definitely spread themselves way too thinly for your liking.

Gemini is one of the intellectual or air signs of the zodiac and, although you enjoy the sort of banter that Gemini has to offer, you'll soon be asking yourself, 'is this person going to put their money where their mouth is?' They are full of ideas but sometimes extremely restless and you know that what you need in love is someone stable and prepared to commit themselves wholeheartedly to the ideal of love, just like yourself.

Gemini is also attracted to you but in a similar fashion may not be completely satisfied by you, either. They are young at heart and need the freedom and variety in life that you may not be prepared to afford them. This is because you have such a possessive and jealous nature that their interests socially may unsettle you and bring out a deeper, darker element of your personality.

Sometimes you feel as if Gemini is simply teasing you and not really interested in taking the relationship into a more committed realm. At times you want it to be free and easy, like their approach, but then at other times you'd like more of a concrete idea of where your love life is taking you. This will be a roller-coaster ride for you.

Because of their fancy flights of imagination, you can expect an exciting time sexually with your Gemini partner. But, when all is said and done, you realise that there's more to love than purely physical interaction.

There is a bunch of Geminis born between the 22nd of May and the 1st of June who are extremely witty and charming and these individuals attract you. You'd like to see a little more heart, not just head, with these individuals and, although they have a superb way of expressing themselves, you wonder whether or not they are capable of expressing their emotional needs sufficiently.

You like to spend money on Geminis born between the 2nd and the 12th of June. There's something about them that presses your compassionate, generosity button. However, you need to be a little careful here because these individuals live for the moment, while you prefer to keep your future security in mind, especially financial security. Apart from this, a working relationship with them will go well and the two of you will get much done.

With Geminis born between the 13th and the 21st of June, you'll explore life and develop many new interests and hobbies with them. These Geminis will bring out the more progressive aspects of your personality because they have the quality of Aquarius and the planet Uranus ruling them. They are thinkers, and you like people who use their minds. If anything, this will be an exciting friendship, even if it doesn't last. You may as well enjoy it.

SCORPIO + CANCER
Water + Water = Deluge

The water signs of Scorpio and Cancer make one of the more favourable love combinations of the zodiac.

You exhibit strength, commitment and a depth of feeling that Cancer admires, looks up to and feels empowered by. But to you, Cancer is a soft place to land in this world of fickleness. They know how to treat you by loving you in just the way that you need.

Cancer is one of the more emotional signs of the zodiac. Being as loyal as they are, they are less likely to bring out any of your darker possessive or resentful energies. You therefore feel peaceful and contented in the company of your Cancerian partner.

You have an eye for detail and, might I say, can be sometimes hypercritical. This is a point that needs to be checked in your relationship with the soft and sensitive Cancer. Although there's considerable compatibility between you, naturally there are times when you'll perceive the shortcomings and flaws in each other. After all, we are only human. You must tread carefully when pointing out these faults to Cancer. Your caustic tongue will cut Cancer to shreds and, if the wounds are deep enough, they may never recover. If you are careful in these instances, you will be rewarded. Cancer is flexible enough to change and accommodate your needs.

Cancer is moody, even more so than you, Scorpio. You'll need to learn to deal with these fluctuations in temperament. Like the Moon that rules them, the tides of their emotions come in and out and therefore you'll always be kept on your toes trying to second-guess their next emotional move.

You have a strong sexual and magnetic connection between you. The energy of your love and compassion flows in both directions, so you'll enjoy each other's sexual and emotional rapport. With Cancer also paying a great deal of attention to home and family needs, this will most likely become an enduring relationship because you too favour a strong base of domestic security.

Lovemaking between Scorpio and Cancer is extremely fulfilling. This may surprise you because, although Cancer may not be quite as sexually passionate as you would at first hope, their soft, nurturing ways will more than compensate for these other purely lustful needs.

If you connect with a Cancer born between the 22nd of June and the 3rd of July, you must realise that they are not quite as strong as you. You will be called upon to help support them and build their confidence, at least in the initial stages of your relationship. Your destiny together is spiritual and you have much work to do to help build each other's character and grow together as a unit.

Cancers born between the 4th and the 13th of July are powerfully attracted to you. They under- stand your deep, complicated emotional nature but can satisfy you. You'll feel attracted to each other from day one.

If you want loads of fun, Cancers born between the 14th and the 23rd of July are likely to satisfy you in this respect. They love the social life and teach you how to have a great time. This too is a great relationship.

SCORPIO + LEO
Water + Fire = Steam

Scorpio and Leo are two of the most powerful star signs, so it's no wonder that from time to time these two children of the zodiac will attract each other—and powerfully at that.

But be warned, Scorpio: Leo is a show-off and likes the adulation and attention of many people, not just you. Playing second-fiddle to a whole lot of other people, standing in line for your Leo's attention, is not your idea of a good time and you'll soon let them know it.

It is you who likes to be the centre of attention; the central figure in the life of someone you consider worthy of your love. If you don't have 100 per cent of their attention, the nasty side of your nature can come out, or perhaps the relationship won't even get to first base.

You're sexually attracted to each other. Leo is flamboyant, attractive and also dramatic in the way they present themselves—in terms of their character and the way they dress and socially conduct themselves in public. You like someone with so much strength and power, but this may be a double-edged sword.

Leo likes to dominate as well, which won't sit well with you. Just realise that Leo's totem, the lion, is the king of the jungle and also the royal sign of the zodiac. This is one star sign to whom you're going to have to surrender some of your power. But as long as you feel this is a relationship of equality, then it's likely you'll be prepared to make some concessions.

Both Scorpio and Leo are protective, loyal and loving signs of the zodiac. Therefore, if you're able to sustain your love for each other, family life will be excellent and the two of you can nurture your family side by side and treat each other with dignity.

With Leos born between the 24th of July and the 4th of August, you have to accommodate their egos because they are rather opinionated, if not domineering individuals. This will irritate you and it's not likely the relationship will last long. Either you or they will have to become more submissive for this relationship to continue.

You have a deeper insight into life and nature, and your definition of power and control is not quite the same as Leo. They are more outgoing and like to strut the stage of life. This is particularly strong in Leos born between the 5th and the 14th of August, who are sometimes exaggerative and belligerent in nature. This may be a difficult relationship if you become involved with them.

Those Leos born between the 15th and the 23rd of August are quite well suited to a long-term relationship with you because their temperament tends to be a little more in line with yours.

SCORPIO + VIRGO
Water + Earth = Mud

One side of the Scorpio nature not often brought up in books is that you like to help people; to goad them on to bigger and better things and help them realise their true potential as human beings. This is the case in your relationship with Virgo.

Virgo, being shy and modest in many ways, often prefers to remain in the background, serving and acting as a support for others. You'll quickly see the true potential in your Virgo mate and will want to help them become the best they can. Now, that's okay, but you mustn't push too hard, even if your intentions are for the best. If you overestimate too quickly Virgo's ability to come out of their shell, you might create the opposite effect and not get the outcome you desired. Try to be patient and enjoy and accept Virgo for who they are, at least initially, until they warm to you and become more confident that your help can indeed be of value to them.

You are deep and complex and Virgo's analytical approach may be at a loss to understand you fully. After all, you are an emotional water sign, whereas they are an intellectual earth sign. This can cause them to become baffled by you, so they must learn to relate to you heart to heart rather than head to head.

Scorpio and Virgo do have some wonderful mutual communication skills. They understand each other and are particularly well suited if their hobbies and interests are similar. You'll spend hours sharing the minute details of your inspirations, motivating each other further in your friendship.

As I said, Virgo is about serving, helping and supporting others. In family life, such sacrifices are essential. If this is what you desire, you will find that Virgo is perfectly able to fulfil these needs in your life. You'll feel secure and grounded with these individuals and, even if there are some problems along the way, the Virgo and Scorpio match is often one that lasts a long time.

You're a little apprehensive about involving yourself with Virgos born between the 24th of August and the 2nd of September. Their personalities are quite different to yours and so you can expect the odd confrontation or two now and then. There may also be a considerable age or cultural difference between you, which can also make the relationship challenging.

Virgos born between the 3rd and the 12th of September offer you a stop–start sort of relationship. It's best not to mix business with pleasure with these individuals because there are some indications that finances may be at the heart of some of your problems.

In a relationship with Virgos born between the 13th and the 23rd of September, long-term love and commitment will be the foundation of your relationship. These individuals' ruling planets are powerfully lucky for you and influence your destiny favourably. There's a mutual attraction and both of you can look forward to a bright future together.

SCORPIO + LIBRA

Water + Air = Rain

Many Scorpios are attracted to Libra, and vice versa, but the sensitive and refined Libra is often unable to deal with the critical, deep and dark mind of Scorpio. For some reason, you feel a need to control and improve Libra, and not surprisingly, they see this as an insult.

Libra is ruled by the scales of justice, so many people mistakenly believe they are quite calm, balanced and harmonious. They certainly strive to be, but they are often struggling to find that balance in their own lives. You must be careful not to push them over the edge by trying to enforce balance on them. Give them a little room to breathe, time to adjust themselves to your intense ways, and the other aspects of this relationship will start to work well for you.

Because of the indecisive nature of Libra—the fact that they are ruled by the element of moving air—you may feel frustrated that Libra can't come to a conclusion. This may be the case when you first meet them and ask them whether or not they'd like to pursue a relationship with you. You'll be at your wits' end three months down the track when they still haven't given you a firm answer. Unfortunately, this is part and parcel of the Libran character.

What Libra lacks in decisiveness, they more than make up for in charm and elegance. They have strong social skills and you respect this in them and enjoy their company.

Libra flits from one relationship to another and probably has a personal 'black book' as thick as the epic War and Peace. This doesn't sit comfortably with you. But if you're planning to take your Scorpio–Libra relationship to the next level, you'll need to grin and bear it until your Scorpionic ways win them over and elicit the commitment from them that you so desire.

Sexuality between Scorpio and Libra is powerful due to the fact that you are ruled by Pluto, Mars and Venus. Intense, exploratory, sensual and fun. What more could you ask for?

Be on your guard if you choose to become involved with a Libran born between the 24th of September and the 3rd of October. Your finances could get rather messy because your approach to the way money is handled is very, very different. Once you have a clear idea of each other's needs and expectations, you can move forward. But never borrow or loan to each other.

Librans born between the 4th and the 13th of October sometimes have their head in the clouds. Indecision in these characters is an understatement, but this is where you can take the reins of power and show them how it's done. You need to give them proper guidance and they will entrust many of the bigger decisions to you.

With Librans born between the 14th and the 23rd of October, you can expect great camaraderie. They will support and love you and this is a great match, especially in terms of your communications and sharing of ideas.

SCORPIO + SCORPIO
Water + Water = Deluge

Well, Scorpio, if you're tired of the sugar-sweet, superficial and lacklustre relationships you might have had with other signs of the zodiac, you can always consider a romance with someone born under your own sign. But brace yourself! This is going to be one of the most intense and also profoundly life-changing relationships likely to happen to you.

One of the key words for a Scorpio–Scorpio relationship would be 'stamina'. Sexually, emotionally, mentally and spiritually, you both drive each other, push each other to the limits of human endurance. This is, after all, what your star sign stands for. Yes, sexual passion is one of the fundamental basics of your relationship. But it is intimacy, a merging of your minds and souls for the purpose of self-transformation, which is really the lifeblood of this relationship. Together your sexual appetites will quite likely be fulfilled, but only because your Scorpio partner understands what other important aspects of love tie in with it.

There are several different kinds of Scorpio, and you should be careful which one you want to get close to. The lower types are addicted to sensuality, self-indulgence and other less than noble human traits and activities. The more evolved Scorpios aspire to spiritual liberation, self-actualisation and human compassion. If the two of you are on the higher path, this can be a remarkable relationship that inspires you on each and every level.

I mention these different qualities in Scorpio because you are both so possessive and jealous that, if you exhibit these traits, the poisonous tails of the scorpion can not only sting, but kill. You need to bring these destructive forces of nature under control and aspire to the highest good in your relationship together.

Scorpios born between the 24th of October and the 2nd of November are instantly attracted to you. The sexual appeal between these sets of Scorpios is heightened because of this. You'll become intimately involved in each and every aspect of each other's life once you connect with these Scorpios.

The best combination of Scorpios is with those born between the 3rd and the 12th of November. Neptune, Jupiter and Pisces strongly sway these individuals and therefore they are idealistic, compassionate and unconditional in giving their love. You'll feel fulfilled in a relationship with them.

There's a gentler and more emotional relationship with Scorpios born between the 13th and the 22nd of November. Soft yet moody Cancerian energies filter through their personalities and make them particularly emotional types. These people are the caregivers of the zodiac and are very family orientated. If you want children and a quiet family life, these Scorpios will satisfy you 100 per cent.

SCORPIO + SAGITTARIUS
Water + Fire = Steam

You wonder how Sagittarius can be so free, easy and unconcerned with things, living in the moment and loving it! But while you're tantalised by these progressive and magnanimous individuals, they scare you as well because your need for power and control seems to slip through your fingers when you're around them. You need to keep a lid on this feeling. Sagittarius can unsettle you tremendously with respect to these primary elements of your Scorpionic nature.

Sagittarius speaks idealistically about love, and you like that. But when you see them operate on a practical level, you start to have second thoughts; doubts that they are as idealistic—or should I say as committed—as you would like them to be. You want the knowledge and security that Sagittarius will give you constant and exclusive love. Often, if you observe them, they seem more casual in their approach to relationships and this bothers you tremendously. This is when your secretive and jealous streak is likely to emerge and scare them away. Sagittarius is another sign that finds these types of attitudes a little hard to deal with.

If you sense that your Sagittarius needs to roam, explore and play the adventurer of the zodiac, you may try a different approach with them. Why not pack your bags and travel as a couple? This way, they can satisfy their need to explore the world, and you can feel more connected to them on their adventure. This will also inspire them and draw them closer to you.

The planets that rule Scorpio and Sagittarius are very friendly and therefore the overall assessment of your relationship together is positive. Sagittarius is frank and open in both their discussions and sharing of ideas, and you like this about them. But likewise you must open up and not be too secretive, otherwise this will scare them away. And, of course, sex is about communication as well. By being genuinely, mutually open and sharing in this relationship, your sexual lives together will be so much more fulfilling, too.

You have a professional connection with Sagittarians born between the 23rd of November and the 1st of December, and it is likely to be a successful one. You should prepare yourself for financial success and enjoy the lurks and perks that come with it.

With Sagittarians born between the 2nd and the 11th of December, you have a great connection, because Mars also rules them somewhat and gives you a particularly close physical and sexual relationship. You're very well matched as a couple.

Becoming attached to a Sagittarian born between the 12th and 22nd of December is not a particularly great idea because your egos are in conflict. They are strong-willed and often very ego-centric people, whose competitive urges will come to the fore in a relationship with you. Your diplomatic skills may not be sufficient to keep this relationship out of troubled waters.

SCORPIO + CAPRICORN
Water + Earth = Mud

Some Scorpios are withdrawn, secretive and brooding. You might think this would mirror the solitary, inwardly drawn mentality of the typical Capricorn perfectly. No, it doesn't, because they are different types of introversion.

Scorpio, you use introversion more as a tactic in becoming the consummate conversationalist, enticing and wooing anyone within your orb. Capricorn, on the other hand, is solitary by nature and sometimes a little depressing in your estimation. At least, it seems like this on the surface. But with a little bit of time and effort on your part, you'll see there's actually a deeper side to Capricorn which, once revealed, is quite a bright blessing for a relationship between you. You see, the water and earth signs do have a tendency to gravitate towards each other and can be quite successful in love.

It's probably hard to believe that Capricorn, in some strange way, enjoys your possessive traits. Being security conscious, both financially and emotionally as well, makes them enjoy feeling needed and being the centre of attention.

Sexually, however, this is a relationship that needs time. You, Scorpio, are uninhibited, forceful and lustful in your sexual attitudes. Capricorn is conservative and likes to play the waiting game. Patience is in order if you want to bring out the best sexual and romantic flavours of your Capricorn partner.

Because Capricorn is so adept at making money and you have the capacity for sustained, hard work, it's quite likely the two of you will be successful financially. As long as you can avoid a monotonous lifestyle, the relationship can develop and mature over time.

Capricorns born between the 23rd of December and the 1st of January tend to constrict you and therefore you don't feel comfortable in a relationship with them. They have an extra strong Saturnine energy ruling them, which makes them particularly conservative in both a material and emotional sense. You don't find such energy easy to deal with.

Capricorns born between the 2nd and 10th of January are, on the other hand, a good match for you because warm, sensual and loving Venus has a powerful influence over them. You'll be surprised to learn just how affectionate these Capricorns are and you'll connect with this instantaneously.

If you're looking for a great friendship then look no further than the Capricorn born between the 11th and the 20th of January. You need to delve a little deeper to get to the true Capricorn within these individuals because there are probably two different sides to their character; one being outgoing and the other quite introverted. A bit like looking in the mirror, isn't it, Scorpio?

SCORPIO + AQUARIUS
Water + Air = Rain

Be careful you don't miss the mark with an Aquarian lover, Scorpio. You might be misled into believing their intense emotional and sexual reciprocation is an indication of their commitment to you. But Aquarius is experimental and may be doing this just to see what being with you is like. They're interested in developing and broadening their horizons and you may simply be one of their emotional experiments.

For this reason, it's important to understand the true nature of Aquarius before getting too involved with them. At times they seem aloof and detached in love, whereas you are particularly sexual, passionate and intense. If you get lost in these emotions, you may overlook the true motivation for why Aquarius has become involved with you in the first place.

Scorpio and Aquarius are fixed signs, which means you're both rather rigid in your opinions and inflexible. Some might even say you're both extremely stubborn. Sticking to your viewpoints means there's very little scope for adjusting to each other's ideas. You can learn from each other; but if you dig your heels in, the relationship is not likely to grow. Be more flexible and accept that you each have something to contribute to the other's knowledge and growth path.

Just when you think things are settling down and you're getting to understand your Aquarian partner, their ruling planet Uranus will completely blow that apart, pushing Aquarius into their freedom-loving mode. This can greatly unsettle you and makes you feel highly sceptical about the prospects of a long-term relationship together.

Aquarius is eccentric, while you need security. They like freewheeling, hippy-style relationships, especially if they're in the prime of their lives. You'll need to get your head around this if you want a lasting relationship with them.

You disapprove of the Aquarian kind of individuality, but you should talk with them about this if you've fallen in love. You need to let them know how you feel. They too may share with you some of the deeper reasons for their need for complete and unbridled independence. Love has to be unconditional, otherwise it's not going to work.

Aquarians born between the 21st and the 31st of January are very restless people. 'Change' is their second name and their opinions are also quite difficult to understand. Like you they are also quite demanding and explosive in nature, therefore your relationship with them may not always be smooth sailing.

If you like quirky communication, you can team up with an Aquarian born between the 1st and the 8th of February. However, this too may be a complicated relationship due to the fact that they have little regard for convention or your concept of security.

Believe it or not, Aquarians born between the 9th and 19th of February may actually be an excellent choice for romance and even marriage. Being influenced by Venus and Libra makes them not only intellectual but also sensual, emotional and caring. They can fulfil your needs and are sensitive to your intimate expressions.

SCORPIO + PISCES
Water + Water = Deluge

You, Scorpio, can become the anchor for the idealistic Pisces. Both of you are water signs and this can be viewed as one of the most perfect combinations of the zodiac. But, saying it's perfect in no way means there won't be any challenges to confront you.

Pisces is indecisive, mystical, idealistic and also at times hard to reach mentally. They seem to live in a world of their own and, while this attracts you on one level, it also frustrates you on another.

Amid this rather nebulous air of sensual and spiritual energy, Pisces is unconditional in their love, which is the thing that draws you to them most. And, without even talking, they understand each and every one of your needs. They are somehow connected to you—karmically, spiritually—perhaps from some previous life. You feel it somewhere deep within you, even though you may not be able to explain it.

Your relationship with Pisces may occur in a time in your life when you need some sort of spiritual or emotional regeneration. Pisces will emerge out of the confusion of your life to help show you the way. But in a similar fashion, you'll be there to help them. You have a forceful, direct and practical nature essential for Pisces to develop in their own lives. You can bring them back down to Earth and help them make something of themselves. As a couple, you can achieve great things together and will always put your emotional and sensual connection first.

At times, Pisces will seem a little unmotivated and this can frustrate you because you're so driven physically and professionally. You must allow Pisces the space and time to develop these aspects of their nature without you riding their backs.

There are strong bonds of love and intense sexual satisfaction with Pisces born between the 20th and the 28th or 29th of February. You have a double-dose of Pisces with these individuals, and their compassionate and spiritual energies will soothe your soul.

A karmic connection with Pisces born between the 1st and 10th of March is even more powerful. Cancer and the Moon influence them strongly and these people will teach you a lot about your emotions and needs. They can fulfil you and also work well in providing you with a happy and secure family existence.

There can be extremes in a relationship with Pisces born between the 11th and the 20th of March because they too have some strong Scorpio tendencies, like yourself. Although this may be a challenging combination, it is also powerful and probably has a better chance of working than with the other categories of Pisces. You can expect an extremely passionate love affair with these Piscean-born individuals.

2010:
The Year Ahead

Life is uncertain. Eat dessert first.

—Ernestine Ulmer

Romance and friendship

Communication, communication, and yet again, more communication! This is your key word throughout 2010 and is indicated by the powerful presence of Mercury, the Sun, Venus and Pluto in your zone of—you got it—communication, as the year commences.

With one of your ruling planets Mars in your most powerful zone of the zodiac, it will be easy for you to make a strong impact anywhere you go this year. Your communication will take several different forms, not the least of which is your powerfully magnetic eyes. But don't let it stop there; you need to also verbalise your feelings if you are to enjoy the benefits of strong, healthy relationships.

Don't be afraid to speak your mind in January. In fact, you'll be somewhat of a wordsmith and can start to realise just how important a word is. Whereas in the past your silence has probably been one of your most formidable talents—and at times, weapons—the spoken and possibly even the written word will play a much larger role in your love life.

During the first month or two of the year, letter writing, catching up with e-mails and connecting with people on a deeper level is very evident. Uranus, the planet of excitement and unpredictability, favourably influences you in your zone of love affairs. Perhaps the type of people you meet will trigger some of these new forays into language, communication and deeper interpersonal psychology.

You are unafraid of showing the funnier, or should I say zanier, elements of your personality throughout February. With the Moon commencing its journey of the zodiac in your area of friendships, it's quite likely you'll have loads of interesting people to meet with and contend with as well. However, don't jump the gun too quickly if you meet someone new. You are more prone to impulsive behaviour and assuming that the feelings you are experiencing are true love, when in fact it may be only a passing infatuation.

You'll be rather motivated in the home arena in February when Venus, the Sun and Neptune combine to provide you with the creative energy to make the appropriate changes in that department of your life. Children will also feature more strongly at this time due to the presence of Jupiter in your zone of youngsters and offspring. Renewed relationships with children, especially if they're growing older and have been a little distant, will be a pleasure.

In March, the planets prod you to look more deeply beneath the surface, especially if you've been mulling over relationships that haven't been going quite to plan. Saturn, Uranus and Venus will all combine to produce a considerable tension and the onus is on your shoulders to find a creative solution to what could be a stalemate situation.

You will feel excited about the prospect of new love affairs, even if you're currently in a situation that is not satisfying you. However, you should exercise caution before throwing all cares to the wind.

Romance continues to occupy your mind and your heart throughout April. With Venus and Mercury tenanting your zone of marriage and your most important love affairs, this is the time of year when love is likely to come knocking at your door.

For those of you who happen to be currently committed in a relationship, you can revive your passion and enjoy the company of each other much more than you have in the past. This is a time of resolving differences and really connecting at the heart level. Some Scorpios are likely to tie the knot in this part of the year and your feelings of love will overflow. You are feeling extremely creative during the months of May and June, but may also be quite highly strung.

Remember I mentioned that communication was the key this year and the month of May will test you in this arena. Talking, not shouting—acting, not reacting—will be the secret of success and the way to smooth over any of the differences you encounter.

In May, the difficult interplay of Venus and Pluto coupled with Saturn, the planet of tests and karma, affects your zone of friendships and heralds a major change in some friendship that has been around for a long time. You'll be looking carefully at whether or not others who have been associating with you are taking the friendship or the relationship as seriously as you are.

You'll want assurances that the love they declare for you is not simply lip-service. There are signs your feelings will be extremely intense, but not necessarily satisfied. If need be, let go of those friendships or relationships that are not serving you anymore.

You have a strong spiritual sense in June with the Moon and Sun in favourable aspect and Venus transiting your ninth zone of journeys and higher learning. You're rather pragmatic, yet philosophical at the same time, and will be in a better position to accept what life brings you in your personal relationships.

This is a great time to travel, to see the world and explore different cultures and meet new people. Some of your friends may even be envious of you, which is due to the difficult patterns of energy, primarily of Saturn and Mars, on your zone of friendships. You may feel uncomfortable being with your usual peer group. Therefore, my suggestion is to break free of this feeling and make the most of what life is offering you.

When the gloss of a new relationship wears off, the reality, the truth of a person's personality, may be staring you in the face, which could be rather challenging, if not confronting. Jupiter exits your zone of love affairs, moving into your area of service, health and daily routine. It could be that the honeymoon is over in some relationships and the hard work of adjusting to each other's personalities becomes a pressing issue.

You are particularly popular throughout July when Venus transits the highest part of your horoscope. You have a strong sense of idealism and the desire to achieve your dreams, romantically speaking. Also, Mars, having moved its position into your zone of friendships, is a strong omen, showing that you'll be making extra efforts to expand your circle of influence and connect with others of like mind.

Sacrifices for the cause of love are not particularly easy throughout August, however, very few people realise the intensity and the loyalty of Scorpio's love. If there's someone who is dear to your heart, you will be prepared to do anything for them. During the month of August, you may just have to do that.

Try not to make too many important commitments. Mercury, the planet of communications and mental activity, moves into its retrograde cycle and you could become confused about your responsibilities or forgetful about what you or others have said. Don't be afraid to ask others to repeat themselves; or if in doubt, leave it out.

In October, you may not be able to pursue your own personal desires as easily as you would like. The powerful presence of Venus and Mars in your Sun sign indicates plenty of passion, plenty of opportunities to meet those who would stimulate you mentally, emotionally and physically. But the Sun and Saturn prove to be difficult in terms of your responsibilities on the home front or professionally.

Jupiter and Uranus further accentuate the fact that you are lucky in love; perhaps suddenly so throughout October and November. An unexpected meeting could result in you encountering someone to whom you would least expect to be attracted. A raging love affair might take place at this time, and again I caution you to balance your emotions with your rational thinking.

You have the opportunity to recreate yourself in November and December while Venus and the Sun are transiting your Sun sign of Scorpio. You'll have a desire to recreate who you are and how others see you. You'll change your 'mask' by way of some new fashion statement, a change in hairstyle, or possibly, if you're feeling radical, even cosmetic surgery for its shock value. In any case, this is a time of the year when you'll want to look and feel your best and will be prepared to do what it takes, spend what it takes, to realise your objectives.

With Mars and Mercury transiting your zone of travels in December, you'll be extremely busy with many interesting meetings high on your agenda. Try to curb waste, especially financial waste, on friends and perhaps even family members who are emotionally unable to appreciate what you're doing for them.

Work and money

In January, you will come to realise how much learning more about your career, about people, and the close interrelationship of the two is important. Acknowledging the link between understanding people and how success is achieved will underpin much of your activity.

In February, Venus, the Sun and Neptune highlight your need for balance between your professional hours and home responsibilities. Your family will need to have you present, to demonstrate your love, but your work could also be calling you, so a conflict of interests may arise. Allocate sufficient time to both areas of your life so that you don't feel as if one is gaining over the other.

February is also a good time for those of you who have been in a legal wrangle. You will achieve a successful outcome or at least hear news that promises a conclusion to some litigation. This could indicate money or a win for you.

March is highly speculative but I suggest you 'hold onto your horses' and wait until April before committing yourself to any wild, harebrained schemes. Listen to what others have to say when good advice comes your way in the months of April and also May. Part of that advice may be along the lines of 'work smart, not just hard'.

Important negotiations take place in June, but you mustn't rely too much on what others have to give you, so much as what you can bring to the table.

If you're waiting for a hand-out, it's not going to happen and may even scare away all your prospective allies in the process. Be mutually supportive and prepared to give as much as you desire to take. This is the only way a successful outcome can be reached.

You're successful in July and again August. Venus and the Sun activate some really lucky opportunities for you in the way of your career. This is a time to take those interviews and meet up with peers and those in the know who can help further your professional life. Profits are also up due to the fact that Mars makes you dynamically capable of capitalising on the opportunities that are presented.

In August, you'll realise that service, the quality of your work, is tantamount to your success. Cutting corners just won't do, even if you do have a lot on your plate. This period can be frustrating, especially with Mars and Saturn in opposition to Jupiter and Uranus, influencing your work and also co-workers. This is a time of team spirit, of not going it alone.

Making radical changes in your professional life in September is ill-advised. Although you feel confident (through the mechanism of Mercury and the Sun) that people will give you a leg up, bear in mind that Venus, Mars and Saturn tenant your zone of secrets and low-key activity. Thus I recommend you plan a little more carefully and don't do anything that is going to upset the applecart or the status quo.

Your finances could be in a tailspin in October due to the rather erratic influence of Uranus on one of your financial planets, Mercury. Don't go spending before you've received your pay cheque. Throw away those credit cards and plan a budget. Even if this is difficult, you'll soon see the benefits and will be able to rest knowing your expenditures have all been allocated well before time. This takes discipline and that will be difficult under these transits, particularly because the passionate combination of Venus and Mars makes you excessive in your spending habits, to say the least.

You have some incredible opportunities in November and, previously where I said that you shouldn't chase or try too hard to achieve something, this month is the reverse scenario when opportunities come running after you. You are attractive, charming and persuasive. Mercury and the Sun give you the right words at the right time.

Those of you who are in careers requiring good communication skills can make a tremendous impact on everyone around you. This will hold you in good stead and give you some extraordinary opportunities that you least expect, due in part to the continued combination of Jupiter and Uranus in your zone of creativity. Much of what you do now will not be wholly and solely centred on what you earn but on how clever, creative and enterprising you can be.

The final month of the year, December, could see you feeling a little down that you've had to tighten your belt and not had the same sort of financial or professional freedoms you normally enjoy. But rest assured that the constraints you've placed on yourself now will only strengthen your self-discipline and give you further opportunities for growth and success. This is a year where you've grown, deepened your understanding, and set in place new foundations for an even more successful future in 2011.

Karma, luck and meditation

Jupiter tenanting your zone of family, inner happiness and family roots hints at the fact that your luck this year will have something to do with digesting your past fully and not carrying it into the future. How often have you entered into a relationship or a new situation, only to discover later within yourself that you projected your past fears and apprehensions onto the new situation? Fortunately this year, Jupiter will allow you to see clearly through your own games, which have been obstructing you from greater success and inner fulfilment.

Mars too is lucky for you, especially in matters of your career. This would have to be one of the best years for most Scorpios, who have worked long and hard to achieve success. Mars transits the highest, most powerful zone of your horoscope for almost six months of the year!

This means that much of your focus is on work and material achievement. But don't forget that this in itself is not going to bring you the karmic and spiritual rewards that you so desire. These outward reflections of success have to be tempered with your inner wisdom and satisfaction from knowing who you are.

When Venus transits the ninth and tenth zones of your horoscope in June and July, take some time to reconnect with your spiritual self. You will discover a new source of energy within yourself that can renew your mind and your heart, giving you added strength of purpose and power to achieve much more.

You could find yourself at a karmic crossroads in September when Venus, Mars and Saturn combine in your twelfth zone of past secrets; also a very strong karmic sector for you. This could require you to digest much of your past or revisit painful memories, which must be eliminated if you're going to grow and mature as a spiritual being.

Don't ignore your creative urges in 2010, especially in October, November and December when Jupiter and Uranus prod you to express yourself and do so in a way that may not be conventional. This is one of the best ways to balance your karma, enjoy life and also magically open new pathways to future success.

May the stars shine upon you in 2010, and may the best of luck be yours, Scorpio!

SCORPIO

2010:
Month By Month
Predictions

JANUARY

Age does not depend upon years, but upon temperament and health. Some men are born old, and some never grow old.

—Tryon Edwards

Highlights of the month

You're on a mental high this month and by the 5th your intensity of thought and purposefulness in communication will be evident to all around you. You need to speak your mind and, if you're not at all happy with the way others are treating you in your relationships, you'll certainly be making your feelings known, and known very loudly at that.

There's every likelihood that you will want to shift the status quo, even if it means writing your feelings down and sending them via an e-mail or calling someone prior to a meeting to clear the air. You can be very effective in tying up loose ends in any of your friendships or personal affiliations.

Between the 6th and the 12th, expect an upsurge of wonderful feelings of affection and love for your current partner or some new person whom you may meet. This is an excellent period in which your communications will strike the right chord with others. Discussions, meetings and other get-togethers go harmoniously and you'll have an appreciation of your own best self and the quality of your friends as well. You have a strong sense of gratitude and will feel as if your loyalty to friends is paying off.

This is an extremely creative period for many Scorpios and, during January, with the continuing presence of Uranus in your creative zone, the way you express yourself will be dynamic, electric and quite unique. There's an air of magnetic power around you, which will also draw to you many unusual people. If you have any problems this month, it will be along the lines of who should you choose to be in your life?

Youngsters also feature quite strongly during this period and you'll be feeling a surge of youth-fulness within your own personality. Some people in your usual peer group could start to appear a bit stodgy or stuck in the past, if I could put it that way. You will want to shake things up, progress your communication and your thinking and, if those with whom you are keeping company seem somewhat 'old hat', you'll be moving quickly to rectify that situation.

After the 20th, home life and family members

feature strongly. You'll be trying to redefine your family role and the role of others within the family dynamic. Mars's influence on your domestic sphere may not make this period altogether easy, but if you're up to the challenge and can continue to utilise your excellent communication skills, you can come out of this with a win–win for all concerned.

Romance and friendship

The lunar eclipse of the 1st brings up many emotional issues between you and your closest partner or spouse. You may have a strong desire to flee the situation but this is not going to solve any problems. On the 2nd, you can talk about feelings and resolve some issues.

Between the 3rd and the 5th, travel, pleasurable pursuits and other social activities are a light relief from the heavier emotional transits of the first few days of the month.

You may feel a little heavy psychologically around the 6th and 7th when the Moon transits Saturn. It seems as if everything and everyone around you is making your work and your home life just that little bit harder. The secret is not to react too strongly.

Your mind is changeable between the 13th and the 15th. A solar eclipse indicates that you may be emotional or moody but still adaptable and flexible enough to walk away from a situation if need be. Short journeys, many communications and discussions will be high on your agenda.

You're very dreamy on the 18th and love affairs take on a rather unreal quality. You could meet someone new around this time and might want to free yourself from the day-to-day affairs of life by simply losing yourself in love. Try to be a little more realistic.

Matters of the home occupy your attention between the 18th and 20th, but after the 21st you have an opportunity to meet or at least speak with someone on the phone who is rather unusual and different from the crowd of people you normally hang around with. This could open your mind to new possibilities in life and leave you feeling quite exhilarated.

Your love life comes back into full swing between the 23rd and the 25th with lots of emotional and sensual opportunities presenting themselves.

Work and money

You probably have far too many irons in the fire as the year commences so it's imperative for you to sift through what's necessary and what's not, especially between the 2nd and the 6th.

Responsibilities weigh heavily on your head around the 7th, but if your planning is effective, you can work through the most important tasks and free up some time.

You are attractive and persuasive after the 12th, with some good opportunities in business coming your way. Use your charm to win the approval of others.

Between the 13th and the 16th, look carefully through your paperwork and the terms of agreement you have with others. The finer print may lead you to a dead-end.

Spending time in solitude on the 19th and 20th will help you clear up a backlog of work. On the 21st, take time out if you're not feeling energetic enough to work the long hours that are expected of you.

On the 29th and 30th, you are emotionally charged and some of your ideas will be well received by your co-workers and employers.

Destiny dates

Positive: 2, 3, 4, 5, 8, 9, 10, 11, 12, 18, 19, 23, 24, 25, 29, 30

Negative: 1, 16

Mixed: 6, 7, 13, 14, 15, 20, 21

Highlights of the month

You're extremely idealistic this month, which can either work for you or against you, depending on how well grounded you are. You're sensitive and need to be with people who can fulfil your inner needs just now. Between the 8th and the 10th, your mind will be fantasising about the perfect lover. You may need to jot down your thoughts in detail, especially if you haven't yet met the man or woman of your dreams.

Creative visualisation is strong but make this meaningful and purposeful, not just an airy-fairy wish list. Get specific with the characteristics, qualities and even physical dimensions of what you want in life. There's no point hanging around complaining that life hasn't brought you what you want when you yourself haven't yet tried to take part in the creation of the circumstances to make this happen.

Work seems to be frustrating for you this month, even though one of your ruling planets, Mars, continues to occupy the most powerful professional sector of your horoscope. You are dynamic, powerful and in some sort of leadership role, even if it's only temporary. Don't let others get you down and, of course, if your idealism is at odds with the reality of the situation, you may need to somehow bridge this gap. Between the 11th and the 15th, you have to be creative as well as have fun when it comes to managing your workload and the people you are directing, if you happen to be in a management or an authoritative role.

You are sensitive to the people you come in contact with, especially in your workplace. You could be confused about how to present yourself, especially if others are dictating standards, dress codes and other forms of etiquette. If you find this too hard to deal with, you could spit the dummy and create even more obstacles for yourself. You'll just have to grin and bear the situation until more favourable circumstances arise.

With Saturn in you twelfth zone of secrets and behind the scenes activities, your best work may be in the solitude of your own personal space without too many distractions. If you're trying to achieve a greater level of efficiency, respect and control, use the energies of Saturn rather than Mars to achieve your goals in February. There's no use getting overly frustrated, shouting or trying to dominate a situation or person. Quietly assertive responses will be received far more easily and this will be the way for you to gain greater respect in every area of your life.

Things turn around rather dramatically for you when the Sun conjoins Jupiter in your fifth zone, indicating that your optimism will be much greater and luck will play a part in bringing you some satisfactory situations. Think big but don't let your ego dictate how you should deal with others.

Romance and friendship

Between the 6th and the 8th, some negative circumstance or a disagreement that you've had with someone can come to a conclusion. This will make you feel much better and you'll be able to recommence your friendship on a better note.

After the 12th, your keen imagination will help take your mind off things that are not so pleasurable; for example, some negative event in the past. By redirecting your attention, you can create something out of nothing and, would you believe, find yourself in an entertaining situation by the 14th.

On the 15th when the Moon conjoins Venus, you have a perfect opportunity to make some new friends but your key word will be 'trust'. If you're carrying around some past hurts and projecting that on others, you may miss the boat.

On the 16th and 17th, an admirer could give you a call or send you an e-mail. It may be someone you least expect and this could catch you off guard. If you're too wrapped up in your work or other personal activities, you might also play down the situation. Reciprocate and explore these opportunities because they could bring you more than you expect.

One good turn deserves another and, between the 17th and 19th, someone may be prepared to help you in exchange for previous assistance you've given them. If you're not feeling 100 per cent, this will be a welcome relief and may certainly ease your burden for a few days.

Between the 26th and the 28th, it might feel easier to throw the towel in if you're just not getting your way in some relationship. Persist. Keep trying and you will come out on top. The month ends on a good note with Jupiter in your fifth zone of love affairs. Some generosity, favour or even a gift may come your way.

Work and money

You have to decide firmly if you perform your work purely for financial gain or it is something you love doing. This will come to a head around the 3rd when you'll realise you're putting in much more than others are prepared to compensate you for. Sacrifice is the name of the game up until the 7th, when a bonus or some additional income is likely to fall into your lap.

On the 8th, you may be confused about your role in some work situation. For fear of embarrassment, you may choose not to get clarification, but that will be a mistake. On the 9th, send a letter or e-mail clearly putting in words what your grievances are and at least you'll get matters off your chest.

Investments are a fine idea between the 11th and the 14th. You have a desire to investigate how you can make money through different sources and possibly even be speculative at that. Seek proper advice before jumping in, boots and all.

Work will dominate most of your activities between the 15th and the 26th, but particularly around the 17th you may be highly strung, over-worked and under-exercised! Make some free time to let off steam and get your body and your mind back in shape to handle the demands of your career.

Quick decisions around the 27th are not advis-able. Think twice before taking a course of action that could cost you more than you bargained for.

Destiny dates

Positive: 6, 7, 9, 10, 11, 12, 13, 14, 15, 16, 20, 21, 22, 23, 24, 25

Negative: 3

Mixed: 8, 17, 18, 19, 26, 27, 28

Highlights of the month

This could be a really fun month if you don't let work get in the road of a truly enjoyable period in your life. After the 2nd, when Mercury moves into the fifth sector, I see a lot of humour, zest and fun-filled events for you. Mixing with friends and relatives will open your eyes to the creative process of doing this as well.

With Venus and Uranus conjoining in your zone of romance and love affairs, it's more than likely some unexpected meeting will take off and bring you a superbly exciting experience.

You could be swept off your feet during this cycle and, much to the dismay of your usual friends, you'll be wanting to spend more and more time in the company of those who are a little bit off-beat and have something new to offer you. Envy is the likely outcome if disapproval is forthcoming from your nearest and dearest. Perhaps the best way to approach this situation is to keep your cards close to your chest because you don't always have to share every bit of detailed information about your life with everyone, do you?

Don't be afraid to advertise your good points between the 7th and the 9th. If you hide away all your good qualities, who's going to know about them? You might feel intimidated at this time, but you must exercise courage and honesty. As long as you do it with a certain amount of humility, then others can gain an insight into who you really are. This is the only way you can make inroads to new relationships and long-term fulfilment.

Mars, the planet that continues to influence your working life, moves into its direct movement around the 11th. This is a great omen, particularly if previously you've been indecisive about a course of action to take professionally. You may wake up and know exactly what needs to be done and, if you've been considering some new line of work, a new position or even just time out from your normal routine, you won't be procrastinating after this date. It's full steam ahead for you, Scorpio!

You'll feel speculative in March and, on the financial front, might be quite daring at that. However, investigate your options wisely before throwing your hard-earned cash at what could essentially be a gamble.

Around the 16th, your mind will be agitated and reactive, rather than cool and methodical in making decisions. Note down your plans and don't be afraid to take your time. Even if you don't get in at the best possible moment, it may just mean you won't lose money. It's better to not make as much as you hoped than end up in debt.

The period of the 17th to the 21st is telling on your health. Don't burn the candle at both ends. Try to establish your priorities and look carefully at how you're spending your time and your resources. You may feel as if you have to pursue many different lines of activity to make sure you don't miss out on anything.

However, covering all bases sometimes means you have to spread yourself too thinly, which could have an adverse reaction on your physical wellbeing. Reconsider your dietary strategies and it may well be time for you to rejoin your local gym and get back into the exercise regime you promised yourself.

Romance and friendship

You're in a playful mood as the month begins and between the 2nd and the 4th you have the opportunity to share the company of like-minded people who are not averse to a good joke, a glass of wine and some entertaining reminiscences.

After the 5th, there may be some sudden infatuation that is hard for you to forget. Your head could tell you that this is not appropriate but your heart and possibly even your body are giving you mixed messages. No doubt this is an exciting cycle but one which may also leave you flat if you can't consummate the relationship by taking it any further. Enjoy it while it lasts.

You have a strong desire to break free of your restrictions and between the 6th and the 11th you might have better luck in gaining more freedom from your responsibilities. If you're a single mum or a person who's expected to act a certain way, this could present some problems. But consider that you can share some of these obligations with someone who's prepared to lend you a hand.

Corrections to your relationships are essential, especially after the 13th. You mustn't dillydally or beat around the bush if you've got a beef with someone. Be straightforward, be direct in your approach, and open and transparent in your communication. What you have to say may hurt the other person but at least your honesty will get the ball rolling towards some resolution, formidable as the result might be.

Don't let money interfere with your friendships on the 21st. You may find yourself in an embarrassing situation, especially if the group decides to purchase a gift that is way beyond your affordability. You must have the foresight to see these things coming so you can sidestep disputes, arguments and any other sort of situations that could undermine your friendships.

On the 27th, you may have an emotional encounter with someone or hear some news that is a little distressing to you. Try to maintain control because you have an opportunity here to guide someone out of the emotional wilderness of their own life.

Work and money

Between the 1st and the 11th, you're active—possibly even bold—in the decisions you make professionally and financially. Work on your house, car and other machinery may further drain your finances, but it is necessary. As they say, 'It's no use crying over spilt milk'.

Quick thinking, new plans and possibly even a timetable that requires a great deal of input on your part on the 18th will work out to your advantage. By managing your time now, you'll have better opportunities to capitalise upon later and can streamline your work and business. This is even more important if you run your own independent company.

Excellent planetary omens around the 22nd between the Sun and Mars provide you with a chance for promotion, future sustained work, and honour and respect from your employers.

The Mars and Saturn aspect on the 23rd is important and helps further solidify this forecast.

Destiny dates

Positive: 1, 2, 3, 4, 6, 7, 8, 9, 10, 11
Negative: 16, 17, 18, 19, 20, 21, 22, 23, 27
Mixed: 5, 13

Highlights of the month

Love may move you to do some very unusual things during the month of April, Scorpio, because its presence in your zone of marriage indicates this will be the dominant theme of the month. With Mercury also joining company with Venus on the 3rd, the first few days will be all about negotiating your feelings, discussing your future pathway with some loved one, or re-establishing the values in an existing marriage or long-term, committed relationship. But don't let this scare you! These are thoroughly wonderful patterns of energy that ensure a harmonious outcome.

If the question of marriage or engagement is posed to you, this is one of the most excellent periods of the year to accept! The combination of Jupiter in your fifth zone of romance, along with this beautiful combination of Venus and Mercury, makes it one of the luckiest times for you.

You are quite emotional, compassionate and

generous this month. There may be no specific reason for you to have to give gifts or share your resources, but you may be prompted from some inner spiritual motivation simply to give of yourself or your possessions. You will feel great in doing this and it will endear you to others.

Between the 8th and the 12th, you'll experience a dramatic shift in your social affairs. The reason for this is the backward motion of Saturn and its re-entry into your zone of friendships. Someone you love dearly may hurt you or you may have a stark realisation of the deeper significance of this relationship. My sense is that a long-term friend may now have outworn their use in your life. I don't mean that this event is based on selfishness. It could simply be that your paths have started to move away from each other and the lessons you were supposed to achieve together have been fulfilled.

This is part of the karmic process of growth and spiritual development. It may not be an acrimonious parting of the ways, but one you feel is necessary due to your changing interests and pace of personal growth. Let things go and don't hold onto them, as this will only serve to create more problems with a bitter ending.

Important negotiations should be postponed after the 18th. Although there appears to be cause for celebration due to the favourable planetary combinations this month, it's still a good policy not to commit yourself in writing until you're absolutely—100 per cent—sure of your position. In business, this may be more pertinent. Any business partnership contracts that need to be signed should be checked thoroughly, and signing along the dotted line postponed until your advisors, lawyers or accountants have had ample time to advise you on the merits of any course of action.

Love, passion and sex are powerful between the 25th and 30th: Venus activates your need for close intimacy and sharing your deeper emotional nature with someone you can trust. In the last few days of the month, however, sex, power and money may be linked as well and could present you with some problems. Honesty and transparency will be the keys to sorting out any problems arising in these areas of your life.

Romance and friendship

Venus is well poised to give you satisfaction and renewal in your love life after the 1st. Mercury also sextiles Neptune, bringing happiness and the fulfilment of your wildest dreams at this stage.

Communicate your feelings; send that little love note or bouquet of flowers to that special person on the 3rd. However, intense patterns between Mercury, Venus and Pluto warn that you shouldn't be too obsessive about your love at this time, particularly up until the 7th. Play the game gently and don't appear too needy in any of your relationships.

The retrogression of Pluto around the 7th is an important factor for regenerating your relationships. Changes to your friendships or perhaps even your marriage if it is now in need of renovation, will happen. This is the chance to clear away all the dead wood and recommence from scratch.

Between the 20th and the 25th, you get the thumbs up on an opportunity to meet someone, possibly through an introduction or a blind date. Put on your best outfit, take along an open heart and be prepared to explore life's possibilities at this time. With the transits being as positive as they are, you won't be disappointed.

After the 25th, Venus moves through your eighth zone of sexuality and deeper emotional commitments. You will not be satisfied with anything superficial in your romantic life. You may come across as a little too heavy and demanding. Try to find out what your partner wants rather than imposing your will upon them.

With the powerful aspects of the Sun to Pluto and Mercury between the 26th and the 30th, you have every opportunity to win an argument through the sheer force of your personality. You may win the argument; but what's the point, if you lose a friend? Try to maintain a balance in all of your interactions as April draws to its conclusion.

Work and money

Saturn re-enters your eleventh zone of profitability on the 8th. This might mean that something you had anticipated in the way of a bonus, additional money or a repayment of a loan through a friend or family member may again have to be delayed a little longer.

Uranus favourably influences your professional arena after the 13th. Sudden events in your workplace or with an employer will work out and benefit you. After the 18th, another lucky aspect between Venus and Jupiter further supports this prediction. Luck is certainly in the air for Scorpios with respect to their professional life.

Between the 19th and the 24th, avoid committing yourself verbally or in writing to the demands of someone whom you work with or for. Hold off until Mercury moves forward in May. This is because you may not yet be in possession of all the facts and could make an error of judgement.

A fortunate turn of event to do with the tax department or a banking or lending authority may be a welcome surprise after the 25th.

Destiny dates

Positive: 1, 13

Negative: 8, 9, 10, 11, 12, 19

Mixed: 3, 4, 5, 6, 7; 18, 20, 21, 22, 23, 24, 25, 26, 27, 28, 29, 30

MAY

Highlights of the month

You're in two minds about your relationships this month, which is probably due to the difficult aspect between Venus and Pluto. You could be torn between two lovers, two pathways, or two differing opinions of friends. How are you to proceed? You may need to retrace your steps and reconsider all possible perspectives before making up your mind.

Unfortunately, if you're operating from a purely emotional basis, this is going to be very, very difficult, indeed. You need to incorporate some of your rational processes to make a firm decision. Much of your indecisiveness will be resolved after the 12th, when Mercury moves forward. This gives you the freedom and the peace of mind to give the thumbs up to either a personal dilemma or one associated with your professional or contractual obligations.

You could feel as if you're in no man's land this month and, if you haven't been given the correct instructions on how to proceed in some project at work, it could leave you feeling devitalised. If you're intimidated by someone more powerful than you, you're likely to refrain from asking the correct questions for fear of being ridiculed or looking like an idiot.

Yet again, you must put aside your ego, humble yourself and be prepared to ask the right questions. This is more a matter of the way in which you approach the person in question and asking sensible advice or pertinent guidance.

Many issues will emerge surrounding finances, methods of banking, taxation, and other shared resources. Hopefully you've had in place the appropriate systems and procedures for dealing with these issues in a timely fashion. If your filing system or your accounting procedures are topsy-turvy, you could be left in a state of confusion, especially between the 19th and the 23rd.

Do you have all your receipts in order? Have you conveniently sidestepped the issue of paying your taxes on time? You can't avoid these forever and these lapses on your part will be subtly eroding your peace of mind and your efficiency on all levels of your functioning, day-to-day life.

So, Scorpio, put these matters to bed while the Sun is in your eighth zone of shared resources. By the 27th you'll have peace of mind if you set aside sufficient time to get a plan in order. Important meetings and information regarding these matters will be high on your agenda.

Romance and friendship

Mercury, direct in its action between the 1st and the 12th, is favourable to discussions, agreements and any other sort of negotiation. If you're a family person, a homemaker or working from home, this is equally important for you in terms of conveying your message clearly and gaining the support you need from your loved ones.

Lighten up around the 15th. You can still be serious about what you have to say without being sombre. Use some humour to get people onside. You're lucky again after the 18th so you don't need to work overly hard to convince people of your position or to get them to give you a little more love and attention. Let the power of your own star sign shine through everything you do and use that as a magnet to draw to you what you feel you need.

Love reaches idealistic heights between the 19th and the 22nd. A secret rendezvous, an exciting affair of the heart or a new friendship may have you disregarding other facets of your life to enjoy the intensity of this new relationship. However, don't ignore your own personal physical and emotional needs because the influence of Uranus on your zone of health may suddenly adversely affect your well-being around the 28th.

Lucky Venus brings with it further opportunities to schmooze socially around the 31st. You mustn't refuse an invitation, even if you feel those who are inviting you are rather boring. Far from it;

the company you'll meet will be rather exciting and most interested in what you have to offer.

Work and money

Your ruling planets are extraordinarily powerful in May and give you a prime opportunity to prove what you can achieve in your professional life. Don't say no to an offer that might sound too far-fetched to be true. It will be a genuine chance to better yourself.

Convey your needs after the 2nd. You can do so forcefully but with grace and tact at the same time. You can push through your agenda and have the support of someone in a superior position.

The settlement of any legal matters or financial or investment portfolios can occur this month due to the favourable influence of Venus. Particularly between the 15th and the 19th, your advisors will act on your behalf to reach favourable outcomes.

On the 21st and again on the 27th you may receive some uplifting news regarding monies that are outstanding. Don't share this information with too many other people because their envy might make you feel insecure about the fact.

Your ego is strong on the 30th, so be careful around this time, otherwise you're likely to embroil yourself in differences of opinion and possibly serious disputes.

Destiny dates

Positive: 1, 3, 4, 5, 6, 7, 8, 9, 10, 11, 12, 16, 17, 18, 27, 31

Negative: 23, 28, 30

Mixed: 2, 15, 19, 20, 21, 22

Highlights of the month

Saturn's forward, direct movement in your zone of friendships means you now have the opportunity to put behind you any of the angst associated with the earlier topic of resolving friendships that have outgrown their use. Older and more experienced friends are likely to be part of the picture, as well as an important component of the puzzle and the solution in this area of your life during June.

Whereas in the past you may have been a little too proud to accept advice from someone like your mother or father, there may be a complete turn-around and you realise that the breadth and depth of their experience has considerable value now in dealing with your issues of personal friendships. Between the 1st and the 7th, you should implement some of the advice given and do so before Mars enters the same zone of friendships on the 7th.

With Mars venturing into a new sector of the zodiac for the first time in six months, your social life is dramatically energised. You have a new lease of life and will want to make friends, share your experiences with others, and rejuvenate your current circle of friends.

Jupiter conjoining Uranus on the 8th in your zone of service, health and enemies may challenge you through the people you meet. Although you want change and a shift from the status quo, you may be ill-equipped for what life throws at you. Major adjustments may be necessary.

We can't also discount the fact that Mars, the argumentative planet in your zone of friendships, will bring with it its fair share of challenges in the way of friends and their opinions. You'll need to be balanced and judicious in the way you express yourself, especially if you disagree with the philosophies and differing attitudes of those you encounter during this period.

Travels of a social nature are spotlighted in June, but only until the 15th, when career matters quickly yank you away from pleasurable and social engagements. You may have more pressing responsibilities to deal with and you mustn't avoid them, whatever the cost.

Between the 18th and the 20th you may have to sacrifice some time to deal with the problems of a sibling or very close friend whom you consider to be somewhat like a brother or a sister. Injury, emotional upheaval or financial issues, for example, could be the pressing problems that you may need to help this person out with. You'll find yourself in a pressure cooker, balancing your own needs with those of this troubled person.

The lunar eclipse on the 26th takes place in your zone of communications, travels and studies. The nearness of the planet Pluto indicates a revolutionary and transformative period is about to commence for you. Your ideas will change and your methods of communication will be restructured to fit in with the path you have chosen for yourself in life.

Romance and friendship

The period of the 7th to the 9th is an important cycle for you. Relationships will take on a new significance just now and, with the important retrograde movement of Neptune on the 1st, you may be shaken out of your unrealistic dreams of love to confront a situation.

If you've reached a stalemate in your love life, communication will be extremely important between the 10th and the 14th. Your partner may not be quite as amenable as you are to sharing their feelings and this could put up a wall between you. Perhaps the secret is listening a little more at this stage and that will draw them out of themselves.

The prospect of leaving your current social situation or romantic affair will cause you some concern after the 15th. The excitement, the lure of something new, will certainly have its advantages, but you won't be able to help thinking about a possible period of isolation that will ensue if things don't go to plan. You can't have your cake and eat it, too.

Make the break if that's what your heart is telling you to do.

Your creative endeavours pay off around the 20th with the Sun and Neptune giving you the chance to look beyond the worldly constraints of your situation. Your confidence is high and you won't be worried too much about what other people think.

Online dating and other opportunities to meet people of different cultures occur after the 25th. If previously you've not been acquainted with these types of media to meet others and to foster your romantic needs, now could be the time to do so.

A lunar eclipse in the sign of Cancer occurs on the 26th. This is near the planet Venus and indicates that you may discover something about a friend or lover that may not sit well with you. Learning the truth can sometimes be painful.

Work and money

Working long hours impacts on your health. Between the 3rd and the 6th, you may have some signals internally and externally pointing the way to an improved health regime, which includes better nutrition, more sleep and an exercise program. This will help counteract some of the lengthy hours and stressful episodes in your workplace.

Between the 7th and the 10th, Mars, one of your ruling planets, moves to the profit sector of your horoscope, which indicates a strong desire to push for higher pay or at least improved working conditions. You meet with resistance, so get some allies behind you before going into battle.

One person's loss is another person's gain around the 15th. Someone you work closely with may exit the picture, leaving you in a perfect position to acquire a more favourable role within the company structure. On the home front, greater team effort is likely.

You may need to gain greater knowledge of the law or at least the municipal codes of housing after the 21st. There may be some grey areas in the nature of your relationship with neighbours and this requires you to take some action. Be prepared for the costs that will be incurred as a result of this.

Destiny dates

Positive: 2, 11, 12, 13, 14, 25
Negative: 18, 19, 21, 26
Mixed: 1, 3, 4, 5, 6, 7, 8, 9, 10, 15, 20

JULY

Highlights of the month

The professional contacts you make this month will certainly be worthwhile. And you've got charming Venus to thank for this. While this planet is influencing your career zone most formidably, others will find you appealing and will want to help you in every respect. Between the 5th and the 9th you can expect a few new opportunities to open up before you. This will excite you and give you renewed confidence in your abilities and your future professional path.

When Mercury enters your zone of career on the 10th, you'll find communication of all sorts somewhat overwhelming. You'll possibly need a secretary for both work and social agendas. For busy housewives it may be awfully difficult to get anything done because the phone may be ringing and the door bell constantly keeping you running backwards and forwards to keep up with unexpected callers.

111

A hectic time is certainly to be expected until the 12th when an important solar eclipse takes place in your spiritual zone. At this time you'll be prompted to look further beneath the surface of things and to balance harmoniously your inner and outer lives.

A deeper, more probing attitude is evident until the 21st. At this time you'll magically find yourself in the presence of wise people; mentors who can assist you with some of life's more tricky problems. Your philosophy in life could change. You'll be drawn to more unusual cultural and philosophical perspectives and might even decide to book yourself on a journey.

Jupiter will retrogress on the 23rd. Expect a pulling back from your expansive attitudes and drive for success. This doesn't mean things will grind to a halt, but the process of letting go, culling and further trimming off the fat from any of your excesses will be necessary.

Career is again highlighted after the 24th, with greater profits indicated between the 28th and the 30th. An extra burst of energy for those involved in independent businesses will pay off and bring some handsome rewards.

Romance and friendship

You may be thoroughly sick and tired of giving your all to someone who is reciprocating very little. Between the 1st and the 3rd, you'll find yourself in a hair-trigger situation or probably reacting out of frustration. You should get used to the fact that if there are problems that need to be sorted out, you're the one that's going to be doing most of the work.

You should feel some reasonably big changes occurring in your family and domestic lives sometime between the 6th and the 10th. However, some sort of isolation or dissatisfaction might linger for a while because you feel that something is still missing from your life. This can change after the 11th when more objective evaluation can be made and you realise that things aren't quite as bad as you're making them out to be.

Between the 15th and the 19th, you have much more influence than you usually do and your words will be of great solace to someone needing advice. In fact, you will find yourself cornered by people needing your spin on things.

There's a strong flavour of self-discovery, mental exploration and educational curiosity as well, throughout July. Between the 26th and the 28th, these curiosities within you may be aroused so much that you'll investigate the possibility of taking on a new course of study for the purpose of expanding your social circle. On the 30th, some new breakthrough in this area will give you a boost in confidence and obviously the chance to meet many new people.

Your self-esteem is also increasing each day, and when Venus creates a favourable aspect to your Sun sign around the 31st, some unexpected, off-the-cuff flattery will lift your spirits to great heights.

Around this time you may also find yourself in a social situation that opens many new opportunities for you. An introduction is a bringer of great luck.

Work and money

You don't have to ask for too much help this month. It will come unasked, which could be rather surprising, particularly because those whom you'd least expect will want to lend a helping hand. Between the 3rd and the 8th you'll find your burden at work considerably relieved through this assistance.

You could be bogged down with unpleasant paperwork between the 10th and the 12th; you're so busy wading through documents that you don't actually get any work done. If you're researching something important to meet a deadline, it's best to do that outside work hours so you can finish the tasks at hand.

You may need to take some time out after the 17th, especially with Mars and Saturn conjoining in your zone of friendships and self-fulfilment. You may be obstructed by others and it's best not to try to enforce your will. Remain flexible and remember that, in a hurricane, a tall tree breaks but the humble blade of grass sways. You need to be a little philosophical to get through this tough mini-cycle.

Finances are on the upswing between the 21st and the 26th. You have some bright new ideas that can help you become financially better off. Trust your instincts.

Destiny dates

Positive: 4, 5, 15, 16, 18, 19, 21, 22, 24, 25, 26, 27, 28, 29, 30, 31

Negative: 2, 3, 11, 12

Mixed: 3, 6, 7, 8, 9, 10, 17, 23

Highlights of the month

It's always important to aim for a harmonious balance of giving and receiving in relationships. But this month, and particularly between the 2nd and the 9th, you may be feeling frustrated that you're the one doing most of the giving. Far from making a dramatic show of your displeasure, you may bottle up your feelings, the repercussions of which are not pleasant, as shown by the combination of Mars and Saturn in your zone of secrets.

Try to express how you feel, even if you're angry; more so if you are feeling cheesed off with someone close to you. There's a lot of tension in the air. Uranus, Jupiter, Mars and Saturn all combine to contribute to some extremely nervous and tense personal relationships in August.

With Mercury and Venus transiting your zone of friendships, you'll want to gloss over these more pressing issues at home, and chill out with some light, flirtatious interactions. On the surface you'll appear warm, expressive and outgoing, but this will simply be for show.

These uneasy feelings may continue till the 14th when the Moon and Mars combine, so it will be difficult for you to sidestep any confrontations. No, it's probably best to speak about what's bothering you rather than letting it turn into a huge volcanic eruption at this time. Working alone is a safer bet, too, because otherwise you might take out your frustrations on your work colleagues.

A far better time is forecast for you after the 23rd when the Sun enters that zone of your horoscope relating to the fulfilment of your personal ambitions. Friendships are spotlighted, but in a different way now. You won't be using your frustrations as a reason for escaping from your more personal responsibilities at home or in marriage. You'll genuinely want to reconnect with those you haven't had time for, and vice versa.

You may be surprised to get a call out of the blue from someone you thought had forgotten you. Likewise, make the effort to reconnect so that you share what's been happening to you in your world. It may be time to take a short trip, an excursion or even a quick journey, for the purposes of spilling the beans and letting someone else know how you feel. This will be cathartic and will make you feel so much better afterwards. After the 25th you may be singled out for some praiseworthy actions or work well done.

Romance and friendship

Around the 3rd, your focus will be fully on work, health and other pressing problems. You may even need to give up some of your own valuable time to address these issues.

On the 5th you may need to forfeit some of your own personal pleasures to assist someone in managing their own debts or financial situation. Could it be that a younger person, perhaps a child, has been fiscally imprudent? You may have to bail them out.

After the 9th, your emotions may feel a little cool and it could be time for you to take a holiday from relationships of all sorts. Get away for a while by yourself and reconnect with your own needs. This is 'me time' and should last up until the 14th, when Uranus activates your zone of love affairs again.

Between the 21st and the 23rd, there's a real opportunity for you to patch up a troubled friendship. Neither of you will have had the courage, or should I say humility, to approach the other; to let bygones be bygones. This is an excellent time when you or a friend can re-establish the bonds of love and affection for each other. However, don't forget to lay down some new ground rules because you don't want to repeat the mistakes of the past.

Between the 25th and the 28th, precautions need to be taken for your own health and wellbeing. If you're pushing yourself hard, you may overlook your own body signals and could find yourself feeling unwell. Boost your immune system and take some time out to nourish yourself adequately. You may have to say no to the requests of someone who's expecting—or rather, demanding—too much of you.

Work and money

It's wonderful to have grateful people around you, and that's the case between the 1st and the 4th in your workplace. Some of the favours you've done for someone in a professional capacity have not gone unnoticed and you will be repaid handsomely.

Some of your wishes in work can be fulfilled around the 10th. Entertainment is part of the mix at this time, so expect a thoroughly enjoyable combination of work and pleasure. However, don't let a minor setback throw you off course at this time.

Around the 17th you may also receive some additional money but could find that it's going out just as quickly as it came in. Just as you've had your eye on something you want to buy for yourself, a family member may cry poor and your compassion may get the better of you. You'll have to postpone that special luxury item you had your heart set on.

You could be lucky after the 25th when an enquiry into some new type of work or position will suddenly pay off. This could cause a dilemma because you may also want to stay where you are. Study exactly what's on offer.

Destiny dates

Positive: 1, 10, 14, 17, 21, 22, 23
Negative: 5, 6, 7, 8, 9, 26, 27, 28
Mixed: 2, 3, 4, 25

Highlights of the month

When you have your back to the corner, it's some-times possible you'll do things out of character. With the passing of the difficult transit of Mars and Saturn, Venus in conjunction with Mars may spur you on to push yourself to your limits in every respect.

Between the 1st and the 7th there are energies flowing through you and around you that make it difficult for you to control yourself! The Moon causes you to think about passionate and physical things. You may be bored, wanting to try something different in life. On the relationship front, this could cause you to feel extremely dissatisfied, thereby experimenting with the other side of the fence. The grass will most certainly seem greener on the other side, but this is not a time to throw all cares to the wind and take a gamble with the unknown.

Jupiter and Uranus will be pushing you to explore the hidden, untested side of life, possibly even things regarded as taboo in your society. If you can channel this urge into more spiritual activities, you'll gain a deeper understanding of yourself and will be better able to handle the challenges of your relationships and friendships.

By the 9th, when Venus enters your Sun sign, you'll be feeling on top of the world and it will be hard for others to take their eyes off you. It's not that you feel great, so much as you look great! A new wardrobe, a change in look or style, will all contribute to this 'new you'. You'll use this to your best advantage, but on the other hand, don't abuse the power that you have during this cycle.

By all means, the power of persuasion is an extraordinary force to propel you forward in work and even in social circles when you have your eye on something you want. And, you will get what you want. But you may also find yourself in the company of those who are vulnerable, less able to withstand your power, and this could cause you to take advantage of them. Remember the laws of karma, and that these forces will no doubt come back to you with double interest rates added.

It could be payback time after the 23rd when the Sun beckons you to make good your promises to return the favour or settle a financial debt. You may be skirting the issue, but it's best to do tomorrow's tasks today, and today's immediately. Peace of mind seems to be the key phrase for you towards the end of the month.

Between the 24th and the 28th, work and

romance is further transformed by you chipping away at those things you feel are outworn and no longer of any use. Implementing new strategies will help you further improve relationships and create better efficiency at the workplace.

Romance and friendship

You have strong desires for love and your passion is strong this month, but don't expect things to happen miraculously. Between the 2nd and the 4th you will need to make an extra effort to bring out the best in your partner. Kindness, affectionate gestures and serving the one you love selflessly is the quickest way to their heart.

Between the 8th and the 10th I suggest you look more carefully at the integrity of a relative. Perhaps they are not being completely honest with you. On the surface they may be charming but underneath they could be rather cunning and trying to hoodwink you.

Friendships with much younger people bring a great deal of joy into your life this month and after the 16th you have the opportunity of attending a party and deepening this bond of friendship. Your feelings could be easily wounded through the words of someone who is a little insensitive around the 23rd. You shouldn't place too much emphasis on what is being said because the events surrounding this person may be the cause of their words.

There's a potential for conflict but also dramatic change around the 25th. The chips could fall anywhere but it's up to you to take responsibility for your actions and firmly determine which way you want your relationships to go. Use your imagination to create new goals and personal ambitions.

The 28th is a pleasant day that gives you a renewed appreciation for your lover or spouse. Your sense of self-worth is also on the up and up, which may just have something to do with why your relationship could take a turn for the better.

Work and money

Change is in the air this month and you'll feel as if you want to make practical your insights into your career and financial strategies. There could be sudden changes in your job and you need to work with a transformative view in mind. Of course, there can be some mental tensions, especially between the 3rd and the 8th. But if you approach these challenges with a can-do attitude, anything is possible.

It's not a good idea to act upon impulse between the 9th and the 13th. You could be frustrated and, on a knee jerk reaction, will take some drastic course of action. You need to learn to manage the whims and the egos of the people around you for the best results.

Between the 16th and the 23rd you'll be investigating new ways to make your communication flow more smoothly. Try not to be too intense or overbearing in your opinions, particularly if the topic is on politics, finance or religion. It's best to listen and agree to disagree.

Don't feel intimidated when you're asked to demonstrate your ability in the workplace with some specific task around the 25th. A crisis may require you to take the lead and show how capable you are. The environment could be explosive, but it's up to you to exhibit strong leadership.

Destiny dates

Positive: 24, 26, 27, 28

Negative: 10, 11, 12, 13

Mixed: 1, 2, 3, 4, 5, 6, 7, 8, 9, 16, 17, 18, 19, 20, 21, 22, 23, 25

Highlights of the month

Negotiations can bog down this month, and the reason could be because you're pushing too hard. Use your intuition, which you have in abundance, to sense if the person is feeling awkward or pushed. At the end of the day, you want everyone to be satisfied with the outcome.

Between the 1st and the 3rd there may be additional responsibilities hanging over your head. It might seem like a good idea to get the difficult stuff out of the way early. But if this involves steamrolling someone, it's best to let it slide and not push your own agenda too heavily.

You have strong physical drives throughout October but may also be somewhat accident prone. Try to look at the long-range ramifications of what you're doing. Slow your pace and try not to clock-watch too much. Relish the moment and get into what you're doing to try to produce something of quality rather than of quantity. The key words for you are 'creative satisfaction', especially up until the 7th.

A sudden need to communicate your feelings to someone may take you off course, which in turn will distract you this month. It's important to put your feelings into words so that there's no ambiguity about what you mean.

If, for example, you're planning to take a break from a relationship or, in the extreme, want to break it off completely, it's not a bad idea to articulate how you feel and the reasons for your decision. You have to admit that if things are spelled out plainly, verbally, no one can come back to you with any misunderstandings. It's there in black and white, and you can always refer back to the truth of your statements.

The health of an older member of the family may come into question, particularly after the 8th. Hospitals, asylums and other places not all that pleasant but mainly of a medical nature will draw your attention. Some of you may choose to do some compassionate work that has nothing to do with your responsibilities to relatives or friends who may be unwell or needing help. It could just be that you feel as if you owe your community some service, and this would be a good time for it.

Otherwise, this period could be a professional low because the Sun, your most important career planet, shuffles its way through the quiet zone of your horoscope. Don't try to push things, even if they're going too slowly for your liking. Patience, and nurturing your projects to completion will be necessary.

After the 28th there are indications of a revamping of your pay structure or some legal issues that need full attention. However, with the Sun and Venus empowering you after the 29th, you'll still have a touch of that persuasive charm that will help you get what you want with a positive financial outcome.

Romance and friendship

You may feel ignored or out of the loop between the 1st and the 3rd. Your friends will limit you and you'll feel separated from them and your family. But this sense of isolation and loneliness is not a bad thing. It's of short duration and will help you gain a deeper understanding of life. Serious reflection and introspection proves worthwhile.

Friendships abound between the 5th and the 7th; but there are some clandestine indications mixed in here. Morals will be an important aspect of your lessons and challenges during this phase of the year.

It's quite likely you'll be feeling off the wall and in the mood for entertainment on the 11th and the 16th. Unusual happenings will land you some unexpected surprises. Exceptional solutions will pop up in your head, but you must trust what you feel. Remember that this is a short high: any spurts of positive insight mustn't be lost. Write down your ideas as soon as they come to mind.

Your personality may be at odds with others after the 18th. Accept the fact that there are differences in your personality and you can't force your opinions on others. Not everyone is going to see eye to eye with you. Doesn't matter! Don't lose it over conflicting opinions. You could be challenged, so expect a lot of lead (as in shots) heading your way around this time. Act cautiously to avoid accidents and anger.

Your wellbeing and creativity is peaking between the 19th and the 25th. You'll easily find something fun to do that won't unsettle others. However, this means you could be ready to take a walk because you'll be fed up with the daily grind and a rebellious streak emerges within you.

You'll be able to keep your cool between the 28th and the 30th because you have additional emotional control. Even if someone tries to push your buttons, you won't feel baited.

Work and money

You'll be driven to do your best between the 2nd and the 10th and will want to achieve a great deal. Mars stimulates your professional activities and achievements. This indicates that much of your focus will be on making sure you don't leave anything to chance and will fully realise the benefits of your hard work.

Don't spend too much time daydreaming between the 16th and the 22nd because this can cause you to invest way too much time on ideas that may not be practical. However, planning for the future—as long as it is within the bounds of possibilities—is a good idea.

After the 23rd, you may be instrumental in decompressing a volatile situation between two workmates. By keeping your cool you help promote peace all around you.

Your imagination will be extraordinarily powerful between the 27th and the 30th. Trust your intuition as well because some of the feelings you'll have about others will be quite strong. Your vision for a better future is positive now and should reap some wonderful rewards for you.

Destiny dates

Positive: 4, 5, 6, 7, 9, 10, 23, 24, 25, 27

Negative: 1, 17, 18

Mixed: 2, 3, 8, 11, 12, 13, 14, 15, 16, 19, 20, 21, 22, 28, 29, 30

NOVEMBER

Highlights of the month

Avoid financial arguments at all costs this month. There's got to be a better way, Scorpio. Mars moving through your zone of finances, income and material values can be problematic, but only if you get too emotionally involved and reactive about other people's opinions. Between the 1st and the 7th, you'll need to set aside ample time to assess your position carefully and that of someone else with whom you either live or work closely.

Sharing the bills, allocating a fair expenditure on different items, will all be up for discussion. Naturally, people have different opinions about these things, but you mustn't let your anger get the better of you. Calm, fair negotiations are in order and will result in a reasonable deal for all concerned.

Once you've carefully assessed and reassessed these financial requirements, the period of the 9th to the 12th reflects Mercury's influence on you to fill out the appropriate forms and send off the paperwork to the authorities to put these commercial issues to bed. After the 12th, your attention will be back on home affairs, with children also coming to the fore between the 14th and the 16th. Get away from business, from the heavy responsibilities of life, and reconnect with your own inner child at this time.

Jupiter's direct movement on the 19th is a great omen and also reflects some of the financial concerns that you've had finally coming to an end. This is a favourable conclusion to any of those lingering, niggling financial issues that you thought you'd never overcome. You can and will come through this and will now be ready to enjoy other aspects of your life more fully.

Between the 22nd and the 29th, there's a good opportunity for you to approach your employer or anyone else in authority from whom you need a favour. Is it an extra amount of money in your pay packet that you're dreaming of? Do you want some more responsibility in your home? Are you looking to extend your home or beautify your living environment? You don't have enough money? Approach the bank manager during this phase. Indications are that the planets will bless you with a favourable response to any requests for help, money or even inner spiritual direction. 'Ask and ye shall receive.'

After the 30th, for some lucky Scorpios, a new relationship could commence that will sweep you off your feet! At this time it's important for you to be aware that even the sort of individuals to whom you'd normally not be attracted are possible soul-mates in disguise.

Romance and friendship

Between the 2nd and the 8th you'll be able to take charge of a romantic situation, even if at times you may be a little shy in coming forward. What are you waiting for? You can stimulate, inspire and redirect your most important relationship in the right direction. Throw your hat into the ring and allow yourself the opportunity to test your mettle.

Your mind moves into an unusual phase after the 9th. You'll be acting rather erratically, wanting something different and out of the ordinary. Although the people you meet now will be exciting and certainly different to your normal peer group, there may not be that much stability on offer.

If between the 14th and the 18th the people or the circumstances in which you find yourself are somehow obstructing what you want to do, you could be using this as an excuse not to get on with it. Believe it or not, some people are afraid of success. You need to be brutally honest in your self-assessment to see whether or not you're sabotaging your own success and projecting this onto others.

You have to bring up some unresolved issues between the 24th and 27th, which may result in you having to deal with such negative human emotions as guilt, shame, jealousy and possessiveness. If you're in a relationship with someone who hasn't yet quite tied up all the loose ends of their past, this could be a large part of the problem that you're dealing with.

You may have overlooked the possibilities in some friendship and only realise the deeper connection with that person around the 28th. This is a time for communicating your feelings if you genuinely perceive a romantic opportunity.

Work and money

Between the 3rd and 7th the budget you have carefully put together or the plan you've been implementing for some time could go completely out the window. Who cares if you binge on chocolate cake, strawberries and champagne for just one night? If you're going to do that, however, don't carry the guilt around with you afterwards.

On the 11th, use your self-control to get through those tasks you've so far been sweeping under the rug. You know that if you keep doing this, you're only going to create an immense amount of work for yourself at some later date.

Some members of your family are not pulling their weight between the 15th and 17th, which could be part of your abovementioned problem. Take control and arrange a work routine for everyone to contribute equally.

It's important to develop a solid emotional basis for your work, especially if you're in a high-stress arena. You'll gain the real benefits of your career around the 22nd only if you've developed your inner poise sufficiently.

Watch your expenses again after the 29th; you're likely to be frivolous and, in the excitement of the moment, may spend more than you can afford.

Destiny dates

Positive: 8, 19, 22, 23, 28, 30

Negative: 17, 18

Mixed: 1, 2, 3, 4, 5, 6, 7, 9, 10, 11, 12, 14, 15, 16, 24, 25, 26, 27, 29

Highlights of the month

The final month of the year could leave you feeling a little weary and worse for wear, but the Sun and Mars empower you so keep a positive attitude around you, at least up until the 20th, when Christmas festivities commence.

You still have loads of charm and Venus's energy to give you successful and fulfilling romantic social episodes. As long as you don't push yourself too hard, do get enough sleep and maintain a good diet, you should be okay. Otherwise, you may find yourself falling asleep for Christmas dinner!

When Mars conjoins Pluto, your two ruling planets, you will feel completely in sync with your own inner power. You may even make a very firm decision to leave a long-term situation. You mayn't act on this immediately, but your mind will be made up. It appears that 2011 may be a brand new chapter in your life!

Travel is very much indicated by these two

planets, Mars and Pluto, transiting your third zone of journeys. If you don't have the opportunity, or your timetable doesn't have enough room for you to take an interstate or overseas journey, you will still be extremely busy running around here, there and everywhere. You may actually bite off more than you can chew, so be careful not to say 'yes' to too many people, particularly if it involves running errands on their behalf.

Parents of children who were born under Scorpio will also be especially busy around the lunar eclipse of the 21st. Educational matters, additional expenses and other unforseen activities will drag you away from a plan you have set for yourself. My recommendation is that you factor in a little extra time for these unexpected demands of youngsters leading up to Christmas.

By far the strongest planets indicating a successful and fulfilling conclusion to 2010 will be Venus and Jupiter. These planets continue to offer you luck, especially in your personal life. So I say, 'make hay while the sun shines', Scorpio!

Any uncertainties in any department of your life that have been plaguing you should be clarified and cleared up by the 30th, when Mercury, the planet of thinking, communication and insight, goes forward in direction. The final important transit of the year is the movement of Venus near the position of your Sun in Scorpio. All this adds up to a beautiful end to 2010.

Romance and friendship

You will feel confused between the 3rd and 8th. You may have had dreams of being in a different place by this stage in your life and could become disillusioned if the returns on your input are not quite what you expected. You have to keep the faith and realise there will be highs and lows from time to time. This could be the moment when you take stock of your personal situation.

After the 10th you may have to take a gamble on speaking your mind with a friend. This could be rather difficult, but there's no use beating around the bush. Speak your mind, and if what you have to say doesn't sit comfortably with them, well, that's their responsibility. Don't expect the perfect reaction.

Between the 15th and 24th, if there are some areas of your life that you haven't developed sufficiently, you'll be forced to deal with them in spite of yourself. If you're honest enough about all this, you'll find that it will work to your advantage. You'll feel much better about your association with others and possibly, if a new relationship is offered to you, you'll clearly understand what is necessary for success.

Try to curb your mental restlessness after the 25th. You'll be impatient and won't want to wait for others. If you want their support, try to give them the same level of support you demand back.

Between the 29th and 31st, you could be shocked to find that some of the company you thought was aboveboard and ethical is anything but. It will be important for you to assess coolly the personalities and motives of the people whom you meet. If you're relying on the credibility of someone simply because they're introduced to you by another person who is themselves credible, you may be making a mistake. Watch carefully.

Work and money

After the 14th you have full permission to enjoy a few extra glasses of champagne to knock the edge off your tension, with it being Christmas and all!

What you think of the outside world will now become a reality between the 21st and the 26th. You'll be surprised at how quickly the laws of the universe will make themselves felt. In other words, if you think good thoughts, good thoughts are likely to happen, and so on. Take full responsibility for your thoughts and you'll see very clearly that life throws back at you what you are producing through your own thinking processes.

After the 27th, more investigation on your part may be necessary if you're contemplating a big-ticket item. Don't cut corners by buying cheaply, even if you don't feel that you can afford it. Buy quality in the first place, and you'll be assured of less problems in the future.

As the year comes to a close, channel some of your energy into creative work. You can express your deeper self by the 29th and make some contribution to other people's happiness as well.

Destiny dates

Positive: 3, 4, 5, 6, 7, 8, 10, 14, 26

Negative: 30, 31

Mixed: 15, 16, 17, 18, 19, 20, 21, 22, 23, 24, 25, 27, 29

2010:

Astronumerology

Life is playing a violin solo in public and learning the instrument as one goes on.

—Samuel Butler

The power behind your name

By adding the numbers of your name you can see which planet is ruling you. Each of the letters of the alphabet is assigned a number, which is listed below. These numbers are ruled by the planets. This is according to the ancient Chaldean system of numerology and is very different to the Pythagorean system to which many refer.

Each number is assigned a planet:

AIQJY	=	1	**Sun**
BKR	=	2	**Moon**
CGLS	=	3	**Jupiter**
DMT	=	4	**Uranus**
EHNX	=	5	**Mercury**
UVW	=	6	**Venus**
OZ	=	7	**Neptune**
FP	=	8	**Saturn**
—	=	9	**Mars**

Notice that the number 9 is not aligned with a letter because it is considered special. Once the numbers have been added you will see that a single planet rules your name and personal affairs. Many famous actors, writers and musicians change their names to attract the energy of a luckier planet. You can experiment with the list and try new names or add the letters of your second name to see how that vibration suits you. It's a lot of fun!

Here is an example of how to find out the power of your name. If your name is John Smith, calculate the ruling planet by assigning each letter to a number in the table like this:

J O H N S M I T H
1 7 5 5 3 4 1 4 5

Now add the numbers like this:
1 + 7 + 5 + 5 + 3 + 4 + 1 + 4 + 5 = 35
Then add 3 + 5 = 8

The ruling number of John Smith's name is 8, which is ruled by Saturn. Now study the name-number table to reveal the power of your name. The numbers 3 and 5 will also play a secondary role in John's character and destiny, so in this case you would also study the effects of Jupiter and Mercury.

Name-number table

Your name number	Ruling planet	Your name characteristics
1	**Sun**	Magnetic individual. Great energy and life force. Physically dynamic and sociable. Attracts good friends and individuals in powerful positions. Good government connections. Intelligent, impressive, flashy and victorious. A loyal number for relationships.
2	**Moon**	Soft, emotional nature. Changeable moods but psychic, intuitive senses. Imaginative nature and empathetic expression of feelings. Loves family, mother and home life. Night owl who probably needs more sleep. Success with the public and/or women.
3	**Jupiter**	Outgoing, optimistic number with lucky overtones. Attracts opportunities without trying. Good sense of timing. Religious or spiritual aspirations.

Your name number	Ruling planet	Your name characteristics
		Can investigate the meaning of life. Loves to travel and explore the world and people.
4	**Uranus**	Explosive character with many unusual aspects. Likes the untried and novel. Forward thinking, with many extraordinary friends. Gets fed up easily so needs plenty of invigorating experiences. Pioneering, technological and imaginative. Wilful and stubborn when wants to be. Unexpected events in life may be positive or negative.
5	**Mercury**	Quick-thinking mind with great powers of speech. Extremely vigorous life; always on the go and lives on nervous energy. Youthful attitude and never grows old. Looks younger than actual age. Young friends and humorous disposition. Loves reading and writing.
6	**Venus**	Delightful personality. Graceful and attractive character who cherishes friends

Your name number	Ruling planet	Your name characteristics
		and social life. Musical or artistic interests. Good for money making as well as abundant love affairs. Career in the public eye is possible. Loves family but is often overly concerned by friends.
7	Neptune	Intuitive, spiritual and self-sacrificing nature. Easily misled by those who need help. Loves to dream of life's possibilities. Has curative powers. Dreams are revealing and prophetic. Loves the water and will have many journeys in life. Spiritual aspirations dominate worldly desires.
8	Saturn	Hard-working, focused individual with slow but certain success. Incredible concentration and self-sacrifice for a goal.
		Money orientated but generous when trust is gained. Professional but may be a hard taskmaster. Demands

highest standards and needs to learn to enjoy life a little more.

9   Mars   Fantastic physical drive and ambition. Sports and outdoor activities are keys to wellbeing. Confrontational. Likes to work and play just as hard. Caring and protective of family, friends and territory. Individual tastes in life but is also self-absorbed. Needs to listen to others' advice to gain greater success.

Your 2010 planetary ruler

Astrology and numerology are very intimately connected. As already shown, each planet rules over a number between 1 and 9. Both your name *and* your birth date are ruled by planetary energies.

Add the numbers of your birth date and the year in question to find out which planet will control the coming year for you.

For example, if you were born on the 12th of November, add the numerals 1 and 2 (12, your day of birth) and 1 and 1 (11, your month of birth) to the year in question, in this case 2010 (the current year), like this:

$1 + 2 + 1 + 1 + 2 + 0 + 1 + 0 = 8$

The planet ruling your individual karma for 2010 will be Saturn because this planet rules the number 8.

You can even take your ruling name-number as shown earlier and add it to the year in question to throw more light on your coming personal affairs, like this:

John Smith = 8

Year coming = 2010

$8 + 2 + 0 + 1 + 0 = 11$

$1 + 1 = 2$

Therefore, 2 is the ruling number of the combined name and date vibrations. Study the Moon's number 2 influence for 2010.

Outlines of the year number ruled by each planet are given below. Enjoy!

1 is the year of the Sun

Overview

The Sun is the brightest object in the heavens and rules number 1 and the sign of Leo. Because of this the coming year will bring you great success and popularity.

You'll be full of life and radiant vibrations and are more than ready to tackle your new nine-year cycle, which begins now. Any new projects you commence are likely to be successful.

Your health and vitality will be very strong and your stamina at its peak. Even if you happen to have the odd problem with your health, your recuperative power will be strong.

You have tremendous magnetism this year so social popularity won't be a problem for you. I see many new friends and lovers coming into your life. Expect loads of invitations to parties and fun-filled outings. Just don't take your health for granted as you're likely to burn the candle at both ends.

With success coming your way, don't let it go to your head. You must maintain humility, which will make you even more popular in the coming year.

Love and pleasure

This is an important cycle for renewing your love and connections with your family, particularly if you have children. The Sun is connected with the sign of Leo and therefore brings an increase in musical and theatrical activities. Entertainment and other creative hobbies will be high on your agenda and bring you a great sense of satisfaction.

Work

You won't have to make too much of an effort to be successful this year because the brightness of the Sun will draw opportunities to you. Changes in work are likely and, if you have been concerned that opportunities are few and far between, 2010 will be different. You can expect some sort of promotion or an increase in income because your employers will take special note of your skills and service orientation.

Improving your luck

Leo is the ruler of number 1 and, therefore, if you're born under this star sign, 2010 will be particularly lucky. For others, July and August, the months of Leo, will bring good fortune. The 1st, 8th, 15th and 22nd hours of Sundays especially will give you a unique sort of luck in any sort of competition or activities generally. Keep your eye out for those born under Leo as they may be able to contribute something to your life and may even have a karmic connection to you. This is a particularly important year for your destiny.

Your lucky numbers in this coming cycle are 1, 10, 19 and 28.

2 is the year of the Moon

Overview

There's nothing more soothing than the cool light of the full Moon on a clear night. The Moon is emotional and receptive and controls your destiny in 2010. If you're able to use the positive energies of the Moon, it will be a great year in which you can realign and improve your relationships, particularly with family members.

Making a commitment to becoming a better person and bringing your emotions under control will also dominate your thinking. Try not to let your emotions get the better of you throughout the coming year because you may be drawn into the changeable nature of these lunar vibrations as well. If you fail to keep control of your emotional life you'll later regret some of your actions. You must blend careful thinking with feeling to arrive at the best results. Your luck throughout 2010 will certainly be determined by the state of your mind.

Because the Moon and the sign of Cancer rule the number 2 there is a certain amount of change to be expected this year. Keep your feelings steady and don't let your heart rule your head.

Love and pleasure

Your primary concern in 2010 will be your home and family life. You'll be finally keen to take on those renovations, or work on your garden. You may even think of buying a new home. You can at last carry out some of those plans and make your dreams come true. If you find yourself a little more temperamental than usual, do some extra meditation and spend time alone until you sort this out. You mustn't withhold your feelings from your partner as this will only create frustration.

Work

During 2010 your focus will be primarily on feelings and family; however, this doesn't mean you can't make great strides in your work as well. The Moon rules the general public and what you might find is that special opportunities and connections with the world at large present themselves to you. You could be working with large numbers of people.

If you're looking for a better work opportunity, try to focus your attention on women who can give you a hand. Use your intuition as it will be finely tuned this year. Work and career success depends upon your instincts.

Improving your luck

The sign of Cancer is your ruler this year and because the Moon rules Mondays, both this day of the week and the month of July are extremely lucky for you. The 1st, 8th, 15th and 22nd hours on Mondays will be very powerful. Pay special attention to the new and full Moon days throughout 2010.

The numbers 2, 11 and 29 are lucky for you.

3 is the year of Jupiter
Overview

The year 2010 will be a number 3 year for you and, because of this, Jupiter and Sagittarius will dominate your affairs. This is extremely lucky and shows you'll be motivated to broaden your horizons, gain more money and become extremely popular in your social circles. It looks like 2010 will be a fun-filled year with much excitement.

Jupiter and Sagittarius are generous to a fault and so, likewise, your open-handedness will mark the year. You'll be friendly and helpful to all of those around you.

Pisces is also under the rulership of the number 3 and this brings out your spiritual and compassionate nature. You'll become a much better person, reducing your negative karma by increasing your self-awareness and spiritual feelings. You will want to share your luck with those you love.

Love and pleasure

Travel and seeking new adventures will be part and parcel of your romantic life this year. Travelling to distant lands and meeting unusual people will open your heart to fresh possibilities of romance.

You'll try novel and audacious things and will find yourself in a different circle of friends. Compromise will be important in making your existing relationships work. Talk about your feelings. If you are currently in a relationship you'll feel an upswing in your affection for your partner. This is a perfect opportunity to deepen your love for each other and take your relationship to a new level.

If you're not yet attached to someone, there's good news for you. Great opportunities lie in store and a spiritual or karmic connection may be experienced in 2010.

Work

Great fortune can be expected through your working life in the next twelve months. Your friends and work colleagues will want to help you achieve your goals. Even your employers will be amenable to your requests for extra money or a better position within the organisation.

If you want to start a new job or possibly begin an independent line of business, this is a great year to do it. Jupiter looks set to give you plenty of opportunities, success and a superior reputation.

Improving your luck

As long as you can keep a balanced view of things and not overdo anything, your luck will increase dramatically throughout 2010. The important thing is to remain grounded and not be too airy-fairy about your objectives. Be realistic about your talents and capabilities and don't brag about your skills or achievements. This will only invite envy from others.

Moderate your social life as well and don't drink or eat too much as this will slow your reflexes and weaken your chances for success.

You have plenty of spiritual insights this year so you should use them to their maximum. In the 1st, 8th, 15th and 24th hours of Thursdays you should use your intuition to enhance your luck, and the numbers 3, 12, 21 and 30 are also lucky for you. March and December are your lucky months but generally the whole year should go pretty smoothly for you.

4 is the year of Uranus

Overview

The electric and exciting planet of the zodiac, Uranus, and its sign of Aquarius, rule your affairs throughout 2010. Dramatic events will surprise and at the same time unnerve you in your professional and personal life. So be prepared!

You'll be able to achieve many things this year and your dreams are likely to come true, but you mustn't be distracted or scattered with your energies. You'll be breaking through your own self-limitations and this will present challenges from your family and friends. You'll want to be independent and develop your spiritual powers and nothing will stop you.

Try to maintain discipline and an orderly lifestyle so you can make the most of these special energies this year. If unexpected things do happen, it's not a bad idea to have an alternative plan so you don't lose momentum.

Love and pleasure

You want something radical, something different in your relationships this year. It's quite likely that your love life will be feeling a little less than exciting so you'll take some important steps to change that. If your partner is as progressive as you'll be this year, then your relationship is likely to improve and fulfil both of you.

In your social life you will meet some very unusual people, whom you'll feel are especially connected to you spiritually. You may want to ditch everything for the excitement and passion of a completely new relationship, but tread carefully as this may not work out exactly as you expect it to.

Work

Technology, computing and the Internet will play a larger role in your professional life this coming year.

You'll have to move ahead with the times and learn new skills if you want to achieve success.

A hectic schedule is likely, so make sure your diary is with you at all times. Try to be more efficient and don't waste time.

New friends and alliances at work will help you achieve even greater success in the coming period. Becoming a team player will be even more important in gaining satisfaction from your professional endeavours.

Improving your luck

Moving too quickly and impulsively will cause you problems on all fronts, so be a little more patient and think your decisions through more carefully. Social, romantic and professional opportunities will come to you but take a little time to investigate the ramifications of your actions.

The 1st, 8th, 15th and 20th hours of any Saturday are lucky, but love and luck are likely to cross your path when you least expect it. The numbers 4, 13, 22 and 31 are also lucky for you this year.

5 is the year of Mercury

Overview

The supreme planet of communication, Mercury, is your ruling planet throughout 2010. The number 5, which is connected to Mercury, will confer upon you success through your intellectual abilities.

Any form of writing or speaking will be improved and this will be, to a large extent, underpinning your success. Your imagination will be stimulated by this planet, with many incredible new and exciting ideas coming to mind.

Mercury and the number 5 are considered somewhat indecisive. Be firm in your attitude and don't let too many ideas or opportunities distract and confuse you. By all means get as much information as you can to help you make the right decisions.

I see you involved with money proposals, job applications, even contracts that need to be signed, so remain as clear-headed as possible.

Your business skills and clear and concise communication will be at the heart of your life in 2010.

Love and pleasure

Mercury, which rules the signs of Gemini and Virgo, will make your love life a little difficult due to its changeable nature. On the one hand you'll feel passionate and loving to your partner, yet on the other you will feel like giving it all up for the excitement of a new affair. Maintain the middle ground.

Also, try not to be too critical with your friends and family members. The influence of Virgo makes you prone to expecting much more from others than they're capable of giving. Control your sharp tongue and don't hurt people's feelings. Encouraging others is the better path, leading to greater emotional satisfaction.

Work

Speed will dominate your professional life in 2010. You'll be flitting from one subject to another and taking on far more than you can handle. You'll need to make some serious changes in your routine to handle the avalanche of work that will come your way. You'll also be travelling with your work, but not necessarily overseas.

If you're in a job you enjoy then this year will give you additional successes. If not, it may be time to move on.

Improving your luck

Communication is the key to attaining your desires in the coming twelve months. Keep focused on one idea rather than scattering your energies in all directions and your success will be speedier.

By looking after your health, sleeping well and exercising regularly, you'll build up your resilience and mental strength.

The 1st, 8th, 15th and 20th hours of Wednesday are lucky so it's best to schedule your meetings and other important social engagements during these times. The lucky numbers for Mercury are 5, 14, 23 and 32.

6 is the year of Venus

Overview

Because you're ruled by 6 this year, love is in the air! Venus, Taurus and Libra are well known for their affinity with romance, love, and even marriage. If ever you were going to meet a soulmate and feel comfortable in love, 2010 must surely be your year.

Taurus has a strong connection to money and practical affairs as well, so finances will also improve if you are diligent about work and security issues.

The important thing to keep in mind this year is that sharing love and making that important soul connection should be kept high on your agenda. This will be an enjoyable period in your life.

Love and pleasure

Romance is the key thing for you this year and your current relationships will become more fulfilling if you happen to be attached. For singles, a 6 year heralds an important meeting that eventually leads to marriage.

You'll also be interested in fashion, gifts, jewellery and all sorts of socialising. It's at one of these social engagements that you could meet the love of your life. Remain available!

Venus is one of the planets that has a tendency to overdo things, so be moderate in your eating and drinking. Try generally to maintain a modest lifestyle.

Work

You'll have a clearer insight into finances and your future security during a number 6 year. Whereas previously you may have had additional expenses and extra distractions, your mind will now be more settled and capable of longer-term planning along these lines.

With the extra cash you might see this year, decorating your home or office will give you a special sort of satisfaction.

Social affairs and professional activities will be strongly linked. Any sort of work-related functions may offer you romantic opportunities as well. On the other hand, be careful not to mix up your work-place relationships with romantic ideals. This could complicate some of your professional activities.

Improving your luck

You'll want more money and a life of leisure and ease in 2010. Keep working on your strengths and eliminate your negative personality traits to create greater luck and harmony in your life.

Moderate all your actions and don't focus exclusively on money and material objects. Feed your spiritual needs as well. By balancing your inner and outer sides you'll see that your romantic and professional lives will be enhanced more easily.

The 1st, 8th, 15th and 20th hours on Fridays will be very lucky for you and new opportunities will arise for you at those times. You can use the numbers 6, 15, 24 and 33 to increase luck in your general affairs.

7 is the year of Neptune

Overview

The last and most evolved sign of the zodiac is

Pisces, which is ruled by Neptune. The number 7 is deeply connected with this zodiac sign and governs you in 2010. Your ideals seem to be clearer and more spiritually orientated than ever before. Your desire to evolve and understand your inner self will be a double-edged sword. It depends on how organised you are as to how well you can use these spiritual and abstract concepts in your practical life.

Your past hurts and deep emotional issues will be dealt with and removed for good, if you are serious about becoming a better human being.

Spend a little more time caring for yourself rather than others, as it's likely some of your friends will drain you of energy with their own personal problems. Of course, you mustn't turn a blind eye to the needs of others, but don't ignore your own personal requirements in the process.

Love and pleasure

Meeting people with similar life views and spiritual aspirations will rekindle your faith in relationships. If you do choose to develop a new romance, make sure there is a clear understanding of the responsibilities of one to the other. Don't get swept off your feet by people who have ulterior motives.

Keep your relationships realistic and see that the most idealistic partnerships must eventually come down to Earth. Deal with the practicalities of life.

Work

This is a year of hard work, but one in which you'll

come to understand the deeper significance of your professional ideals. You may discover a whole new aspect to your career, which involves a more compassionate and self-sacrificing side to your personality.

You'll also find that your way of working will change and you'll be more focused and able to get into the spirit of whatever you do. Finding meaningful work is very likely and therefore this could be a year when money, security, creativity and spirituality overlap to bring you a great sense of personal satisfaction.

Tapping into your greater self through meditation and self-study will bring you great benefits throughout 2010.

Improving your luck

Using self-sacrifice along with discrimination will be an unusual method of improving your luck. The laws of karma state that what you give, you receive in greater measure. This is one of the principal themes for you in 2010.

The 1st, 8th, 15th and 20th hours of Tuesdays are your lucky times. The numbers 7, 16, 25 and 34 should be used to increase your lucky energies.

8 is the year of Saturn

Overview

The earthy and practical sign of Capricorn and its ruler Saturn are intimately linked to the number

8, which rules you in 2010. Your discipline and far-sightedness will help you achieve great things in the coming year. With cautious discernment, slowly but surely you will reach your goals.

It may be that due to the influence of the solitary Saturn, your best work and achievement will be behind closed doors away from the limelight. You mustn't fear this as you'll discover many new things about yourself. You'll learn just how strong you really are.

Love and pleasure

Work will overshadow your personal affairs in 2010, but you mustn't let this erode the personal relationships you have. Becoming a workaholic brings great material successes but will also cause you to become too insular and aloof. Your family members won't take too kindly to you working 100-hour weeks.

Responsibility is one of the key words for this number and you will therefore find yourself in a position of authority that leaves very little time for fun. Try to make the time to enjoy the company of friends and family and by all means schedule time off on the weekends as it will give you the peace of mind you're looking for.

Because of your responsible attitude it will be very hard for you not to assume a greater role in your workplace and this indicates longer working hours with the likelihood of a promotion with equally good remuneration.

Work

Money is high on your agenda in 2010. Number 8 is a good money number according to the Chinese and this year is at last likely to bring you the fruits of your hard labour. You are cautious and resourceful in all your dealings and will not waste your hard-earned savings. You will also be very conscious of using your time wisely.

You will be given more responsibilities and you're likely to take them on, if only to prove to yourself that you can handle whatever life dishes up.

Expect a promotion in which you'll play a leading role in your work. Your diligence and hard work will pay off, literally, in a bigger salary and more respect from others.

Improving your luck

Caution is one of the key characteristics of the number 8 and is linked to Capricorn. But being overly cautious could cause you to miss valuable opportunities. If an offer is put to you, try to think outside the square and balance it with your naturally cautious nature.

Be gentle and kind to yourself. By loving yourself, others will naturally love you, too. The 1st, 8th, 15th and 20th hours of Saturdays are exceptionally lucky for you, as are the numbers 1, 8, 17, 26 and 35.

9 is the year of Mars

Overview

You are now entering the final year of a nine-year cycle dominated by the planet Mars and the sign of Aries. You'll be completing many things and are determined to be successful after several years of intense work.

Some of your relationships may now have reached their use-by date and even personal affairs may need to be released. Don't let arguments and disagreements get in the road of friendly resolution in these areas of your life.

Mars is a challenging planet, and this year, although you will be very active and productive, you may find others trying to obstruct the achievement of your goals. As a result you may react strongly to them, thereby creating disharmony in your workplace. Don't be so impulsive or reckless, and generally slow things down. The slower, steadier approach has greater merit this year.

Love and pleasure

If you become too bossy and pushy with friends this year you will just end up pushing them out of your life. It's a year to end certain friendships but by the same token it could be the perfect time to remove conflicts and thereby bolster your love affairs in 2010.

If you're feeling a little irritable and angry with those you love, try getting rid of these negative feelings through some intense, rigorous sports and physical activity. This will definitely relieve tension and improve your personal life.

Work

Because you're healthy and able to work at a more intense pace you'll achieve an incredible amount in the coming year. Overwork could become a problem if you're not careful.

Because the number 9 and Mars are infused with leadership energy, you'll be asked to take the reins of the job and steer your company or group in a certain direction. This will bring with it added responsibility but also a greater sense of purpose for you.

Improving your luck

Because of the hot and restless energy of the number 9, it is important to create more mental peace in your life this year. Lower the temperature, so to speak, and decompress your relationships rather than becoming aggravated. Try to talk with your work partners and loved ones rather than telling them what to do. This will generally pick up your health and your relationships.

The 1st, 8th, 15th and 20th hours of Tuesdays are the luckiest for you this year and, if you're involved in any disputes or need to attend to health issues, these times are also very good to get the best results. Your lucky numbers are 9, 18, 27 and 36

SCORPIO

2010:
Your Daily Planner

*In theory, there is no difference between theory and
practice. But, in practice, there is.*

—Jan van de Snepscheut

According to astrology, the success of any venture or
activity is dependent upon the planetary positions
at the time you commence that activity. Electional
astrology helps you select the most appropriate
times for many of your day-to-day endeavours.
These dates are applicable to each and every zodiac
sign and can be used freely by one and all, even if
your star sign doesn't fall under the one mentioned
in this book. Please note that the daily planner is a
universal system applicable equally to all *twelve* star
signs. Anyone and everyone can use this planner
irrespective of their birth sign.

Ancient astrologers understood the planetary
patterns and how they impacted on each of us. This
allowed them to suggest the best possible times
to start various important activities. For example,
many farmers still use this approach today: they
understand the phases of the Moon, and attest to
the fact that planting seeds on certain lunar days
produces a far better crop than does planting on
other days.

In the following section, many facets of daily
life are considered. Using the lunar cycle and the
combined strength of other planets allows us to
work out the best times to do them. This is your
personal almanac, which can be used in conjunction with any star sign to help optimise the results.

First, select the activity you are interested in, and then quickly scan the year for the best months to start it. When you have selected the month, you can finetune your timing by finding the best specific dates. You can then be sure that the planetary energies will be in sync with you, offering you the best possible outcome.

Coupled with what you know about your monthly and weekly trends, the daily planner is an effective tool to help you capitalise on opportunities that come your way this year.

Good luck, and may the planets bless you with great success, fortune and happiness in 2010!

Getting started in 2010

How many times have you made a new year's resolution to begin a diet or be a better person in your relationships? And, how many times has it not worked out? Well, part of the reason may be that you started out at the wrong time, because how successful you are is strongly influenced by the position of the Moon and the planets when you begin a particular activity. You will be more successful with the following endeavours if you start them on the days indicated.

Relationships

We all feel more empowered on some days than on others. This is because the planets have some power over us—their movement and their relationships to each other determine the ebb and flow of our energies. And, our levels of self-confidence and sense of romantic magnetism play an important part in the way we behave in relationships.

Your daily planner tells you the ideal dates for meeting new friends, initiating a love affair, spending time with family and loved ones—it even tells you the most appropriate times for sexual encounters.

You'll be surprised at how much more impact you will make in your relationships when you tune yourself in to the planetary energies on these special dates.

Falling in love/restoring love

During these times you could expect favourable energies to meet your soulmate or, if you've had difficulty in a relationship, to approach the one you love to rekindle both your and their emotional responses:

January	18, 20, 23, 24
February	15, 16, 20, 24
March	29
April	16
May	14, 17, 18, 19, 20, 23
June	14, 15, 16, 20, 21
July	12
August	10, 13, 14
September	9, 21, 22
October	8, 18, 19, 20
November	14, 15, 16, 19, 20, 21
December	13, 17, 18

Special times with friends and family

Socialising, partying and having a good time with those whose company you enjoy is highly favourable under the following dates. They are excellent to spend time with family and loved ones in a domestic environment:

January	6, 26, 27
February	12, 13, 14, 15, 16, 20, 24
March	11, 21, 22, 29, 30, 31
April	8
May	15, 16, 17, 18, 19, 20, 23, 24
June	1, 2, 3, 11, 12, 14, 15, 16, 20, 21, 29, 30
July	8, 9, 12, 17, 18, 26, 27
August	5, 6, 9, 10, 13, 14, 22, 23, 24
September	1, 2, 5, 9, 10, 18, 19, 20, 30
October	3, 19, 20, 25, 26, 30, 31
November	3, 4, 14, 15, 16, 22, 26, 27
December	2, 9, 10, 11, 19, 20, 24, 25

Healing or resuming relationships

If you're trying to get back together with the one you love or need a heart-to-heart or deep-and-meaningful discussion with someone, you can try the following dates to do so:

January	12, 13, 14, 15, 21, 22, 23, 24, 25
February	6
March	6, 31
April	2, 7, 8, 12, 16, 19, 23, 24, 25, 26

2010: YOUR DAILY PLANNER

May	10, 11, 12, 13, 14, 15, 16, 17, 18, 19, 20, 21, 22, 23, 24, 25, 26, 27, 28, 30
June	3, 8, 9, 10, 11, 12, 13, 14, 15, 16, 17, 21, 22, 23, 25, 26, 27, 28, 29, 30
July	1, 2, 3, 4, 5, 10, 11, 12, 13, 15, 16, 17, 18, 19, 20, 21, 22, 23, 28, 29, 30
August	1, 2, 3, 4, 5, 6, 9, 10, 13, 14, 15, 16, 20, 23, 25, 26, 27
September	2, 5, 9, 10, 13, 17, 18, 19, 20
October	1, 2, 3, 6, 12, 13, 14, 15, 20, 22, 23, 24, 25, 26, 27, 28, 29, 30, 31
November	3, 4, 5, 6, 7, 8, 9, 21, 27, 28, 29, 30
December	2, 3, 4, 6, 12, 13, 14, 17, 18, 19, 20, 21, 23, 24, 25

Sexual encounters

Physical and sexual energies are well favoured on the following dates. The energies of the planets enhance your moments of intimacy during these times:

January	1, 6, 7, 21, 22
February	6, 12, 13, 14, 20, 24
March	14, 15, 17, 18, 19, 30, 31
April	23, 24, 25, 26
May	9, 12, 14, 17, 18, 19, 20
June	3, 8, 9, 10, 11, 14, 15, 16, 20, 21, 29, 30
July	8, 9, 10, 11, 12
August	6, 10, 13, 14, 22, 23, 24

September	3, 4, 5, 6, 9, 10, 18, 19, 20, 21, 22, 30
October	1, 2, 3, 7, 8, 18, 19, 20, 23, 24, 28, 29, 30, 31
November	3, 4, 14, 15, 16, 19, 24, 25, 26, 27
December	2, 10, 11, 12, 13, 15, 16, 17, 19, 20, 22, 23, 24, 25

Health and wellbeing

Your aura and life force are susceptible to the movements of the planets—in particular, they respond to the phases of the Moon.

The following dates are the most appropriate times to begin a diet, have cosmetic surgery, or seek medical advice. They also indicate the best times to help others.

Feeling of wellbeing

Your physical as well as your mental alertness should be strong on these following dates. You can plan your activities and expect a good response from others:

January	2, 3, 4, 5, 6, 7, 11, 12, 13, 14, 16, 17, 18, 21, 22, 23, 24, 30, 31
February	1, 2, 7, 8, 15, 16, 17, 18, 19, 20, 21, 22, 23, 24, 25, 26, 27, 28
March	16, 17, 18, 19, 20, 22, 23, 24, 25, 26, 27, 28, 29
April	7, 13, 14, 16, 28
May	2, 11, 14, 25, 26
June	8, 22, 23, 26, 27, 28, 29, 30

July	4, 5, 8, 9, 12, 13, 14, 15, 16, 19, 20, 23, 24, 25
August	5, 6, 9, 10, 11, 12, 13, 15, 16, 20, 21
September	9, 10, 11, 12, 13, 16, 17, 21, 22, 24, 25, 28, 29, 30
October	3, 4, 5, 6, 7, 8, 9, 10, 13, 14, 15, 22
November	4, 5, 6, 10, 11, 19, 20, 21
December	7, 8, 17, 18, 28, 29

Healing and medicine

These times are good for approaching others who have expertise when you need some deeper under-standing. They are also favourable for any sort of healing or medication and making appointments with doctors or psychologists. Planning surgery around these dates should bring good results.

Often giving up our time and energy to assist others doesn't necessarily result in the expected outcome. However, by lending a helping hand to a friend on the following dates, the results should be favourable:

January	1, 2, 3, 4, 6, 7, 8, 9, 11, 12, 13, 14, 15, 16, 17, 18, 19, 20, 21, 22, 23, 24, 26, 27, 28, 29, 30, 31
February	1, 5, 6, 9, 11, 12, 13, 14, 15, 16, 19
March	1, 2, 3, 4, 5, 8, 9, 10, 11, 12, 18, 19, 24, 25, 29
April	1, 3, 4, 5, 22, 26
May	4, 5

June	1, 2, 3, 9, 10, 17, 18, 22, 23, 24, 25, 29, 30
July	6, 7, 15, 16, 17, 18, 19, 21, 22, 23, 24, 25, 26
August	2, 3, 4, 11, 12, 17, 18, 19, 20, 21, 30, 31
September	6, 7, 8, 10, 11, 12, 13, 14, 15, 16, 17, 18, 26, 27, 28, 29
October	5, 7, 8, 9, 10, 11, 12, 13, 14, 15, 16, 17, 18, 19, 20, 21, 22, 23, 24, 25, 26, 28, 29, 30, 31
November	1, 2, 3, 5, 7, 8, 10, 11, 14, 15, 17, 18, 19, 22, 23
December	4, 5, 7, 8, 9, 10, 12, 13, 14, 16, 23, 24, 25, 26, 28, 29, 30, 31

Money

Money is an important part of life, and involves many decisions—decisions about borrowing, investing, spending. The ideal times for transactions are very much influenced by the planets, and whether your investment or nest egg grows or doesn't grow can often be linked to timing. Making your decisions on the following dates could give you a whole new perspective on your financial future.

Managing wealth and money

To build your nest egg it's a good time to open your bank account or invest money on the following dates:

January	1, 6, 7, 13, 14, 15, 18, 21, 22, 28, 29
February	3, 4, 9, 10, 11, 12, 13, 14, 15, 17, 18, 24, 25
March	2, 3, 9, 10, 16, 17, 18, 23, 24, 29, 30, 31

April	5, 6, 7, 13, 14, 19, 20, 21, 26, 27,
May	2, 3, 4, 10, 11, 17, 18, 23, 24, 30, 31
June	6, 7, 8, 13, 14, 19, 20, 21, 26, 27, 28
July	4, 5, 10, 11, 12, 17, 18, 23, 24, 25, 31
August	1, 7, 8, 13, 14, 20, 21, 27, 28, 29
September	3, 4, 9, 10, 16, 17, 23, 24, 25
October	1, 2, 7, 8, 13, 14, 15, 21, 22, 28, 29
November	3, 4, 10, 11, 17, 18, 24, 25
December	1, 2, 7, 8, 14, 15, 16, 21, 22, 23, 24, 29

Spending

It's always fun to spend but the following dates are more in tune with this activity and are likely to give you better results:

January	3, 4, 5, 6, 7, 8, 9, 10, 11, 12, 13, 14
February	3, 4, 5, 10, 19
March	8, 10, 11, 13, 14, 19
April	7, 8, 11, 12, 22
May	6, 7, 8, 9, 10, 11, 12, 13, 17, 18, 19, 20, 21, 22, 23, 24, 25, 26, 27, 28
June	1, 11, 12, 14, 16, 17, 19, 23, 25, 26, 27, 28, 29, 30
July	6, 7, 8, 23, 24, 25, 26, 27, 28, 29, 31
August	1, 2, 3, 4, 5, 15, 16, 17, 18, 19, 30, 31
September	1, 2, 3, 4, 17, 18, 19, 20, 21, 22, 23, 27, 28, 29, 30
October	4, 7, 12, 13, 14, 15, 16, 17, 18, 19, 27, 28

November   2, 3, 4, 25, 26, 27, 28

December   11, 22, 23

Selling

If you're thinking of selling something, whether it is small or large, consider the following dates as ideal times to do so:

January   18

February   12, 13, 14, 15

March   5, 6, 9, 14, 15, 16, 17, 18, 19, 21

April   1, 3, 4, 5, 22, 26

May   7, 12, 21, 29

June   3, 8, 9, 10, 11, 12, 13, 17, 24, 25, 26, 27, 28, 30

July   1, 2, 7, 9, 10, 11, 25, 27, 28, 29, 30, 31

August   1, 2, 3, 4, 5, 6, 7, 8, 9, 10, 13, 20, 23, 28

September   2, 9, 10, 11, 12, 13, 14, 15, 16, 17, 18, 19, 20, 21, 22, 23, 24, 26, 30

October   1, 2, 3, 4, 6, 7, 10, 11, 17, 18, 19, 20, 21, 22, 23, 24, 25, 27, 29

November   3, 4, 5, 6, 7, 11, 14, 15, 16, 17, 18, 19, 21, 23, 24, 25, 26, 27, 28, 29, 30

December   1, 2, 3, 4, 5, 6, 7, 8, 9, 10, 11, 12, 13, 14, 15, 16, 17, 18, 19, 20, 21, 22

Borrowing

Few of us like to borrow money, but if you must, taking out a loan on the following dates will be positive:

January	12, 30
February	7, 12, 13
March	6, 7, 8, 11
April	3, 4, 8
May	9, 28, 29
June	1, 2, 3, 4, 5, 29, 30
July	1, 2, 3, 26, 27, 28, 29, 30
August	9, 25, 26
September	5, 6
October	3, 30
November	26, 27
December	3, 4, 21, 22, 23, 30, 31

Work and education

Your career is important, and continual improvement of your skills is therefore also crucial professionally, mentally and socially. The dates below will help you find out the most appropriate times to improve your professional talents and commence new work or education associated with your work.

You may need to decide when to start learning a new skill, when to ask for a promotion, and even when to make an important career change. Here are the days when your mental and educational power is strong.

Learning new skills

Educational pursuits are lucky and bring good results on the following dates:

January	15, 16, 17, 18, 19, 20, 21, 22, 25, 26, 27
February	14, 15, 16, 17, 18, 19, 22, 23, 28
March	16, 17, 18, 21, 22, 27, 28
April	17, 18, 24, 25
May	15, 16, 21, 22
June	12, 17, 18, 24, 25
July	15, 16, 21, 22, 23, 24, 25
August	11, 12, 17, 18, 19
September	8, 13, 15, 20, 21, 22
October	11, 12
November	7, 8, 9
December	6, 19, 20

Changing career path or profession

If you're feeling stuck and need to move into a new professional activity, changing jobs could be done at these times:

January	6, 7, 15, 16, 17, 23, 24
February	12, 13, 14, 19, 20, 21
March	19, 20, 27, 28
April	15, 16, 24, 25
May	14, 21, 22
June	17, 18, 19, 20, 21
July	8, 9, 15, 16, 23, 24, 25

August	5, 6, 11, 12, 20, 21, 22, 23
September	1, 2, 8, 13, 14, 15, 17
October	8, 13, 14, 15, 16, 17
November	3, 4, 10, 11, 19, 20, 21
December	1, 2, 3, 7, 8, 17, 18, 28, 29

Promotion, professional focus and hard work

To increase your mental focus and achieve good results from the work you do; promotions are also likely on these dates:

January	4, 5, 6, 11, 12, 13, 14, 15, 16, 17, 18, 19, 21
February	6
March	16, 17, 18, 19, 20, 21, 23, 24, 25, 26, 27, 28, 29
April	8, 28, 29
May	12, 21
June	25, 26, 27, 28
July	4, 5, 8, 9, 12, 13, 14, 15, 16, 17, 18, 19, 20, 21, 22, 23, 24, 25, 26, 27
August	5, 6, 10, 11, 12, 13, 14, 15, 16, 17, 18, 19, 20, 21, 22, 23, 24
September	13, 14, 15
October	10, 11, 12, 13, 14, 15, 17, 18, 19, 20, 22, 23, 24, 30, 31
November	2, 4, 5, 6, 7, 8, 9, 23, 24, 25, 26, 27, 28, 29, 30
December	2, 3, 4, 11, 12, 13, 14, 15, 16, 18, 19, 20, 21, 23, 24, 25

Travel

Setting out on a holiday or adventurous journey is exciting. Here are the most favourable times for doing this. Travel on the following dates is likely to give you a sense of fulfilment:

January	15
February	15, 16, 18, 19, 20, 21
March	16, 17, 18, 21, 22, 23
April	19, 24, 25, 26, 27
May	16, 17, 18, 21, 22
June	17, 18, 19, 20, 21, 24, 25
July	21, 22, 23, 24, 25
August	19
September	9, 21, 22
October	18, 19, 20, 21, 22
November	7, 16, 17, 18
December	6, 14, 16, 19, 20

Beauty and grooming

Believe it or not, cutting your hair or nails has a powerful effect on your body's electromagnetic energy. If you cut your hair or nails at the wrong time of the month, you can reduce your level of vitality significantly. Use these dates to ensure you optimise your energy levels by staying in tune with the stars.

Hair and nails

January	1, 2, 3, 4, 5, 6, 7, 8, 11, 12, 13, 14, 15, 18, 19, 20, 21, 22, 25, 26, 27
February	3, 4, 5, 7, 8, 15, 16, 17, 18, 19, 22, 23, 24, 25
March	2, 3, 4, 6, 7, 8, 14, 15, 21, 22
April	1, 2, 3, 4, 5, 10, 11, 12, 17, 18, 19, 20, 21, 22, 23, 28, 29, 30
May	1, 2, 3, 4, 5, 7, 8, 9, 10, 11, 12, 13, 15, 16, 17, 18, 25, 26 27, 28, 29, 30
June	4, 5, 11, 12, 14, 15, 16, 24, 25
July	1, 2, 3, 8, 9, 12, 13, 14, 21, 22, 28, 29, 30
August	1, 2, 5, 6, 17, 18, 19, 25, 26
September	1, 2, 6, 7, 14, 15, 21, 22, 23, 24, 28, 29, 30
October	3, 4, 11, 12, 18, 19, 20, 25, 26, 27, 28, 29, 30
November	7, 8, 9, 14, 15, 16, 22, 23, 24, 25, 26, 27
December	5, 6, 12, 13, 19, 20, 21, 22, 23, 24, 25

Therapies, massage and self-pampering

January	6, 7, 13, 14, 15, 18, 19, 20, 21
February	2, 3, 9, 11, 14
March	1, 9, 14, 16, 17, 20, 23, 29
April	4, 5, 6, 10, 11, 12, 13, 17, 25, 26
May	2, 3, 7, 8, 9, 10, 11, 14, 15, 16, 17, 22, 23, 24, 31
June	3, 5, 12, 18, 19, 26, 27
July	4, 7, 8, 9, 10, 16, 23, 28, 29, 30, 31
August	3, 4, 5, 6, 7, 13, 20, 21, 24, 25, 26, 27, 28, 31
September	2, 17, 21, 28, 29

October	13, 14, 15, 18, 19, 21, 25, 26, 27, 28
November	2, 3, 9, 11, 14, 15, 16, 17, 21, 24, 29
December	7, 12, 13, 14, 15, 18, 19, 20, 22, 26, 27, 28, 29

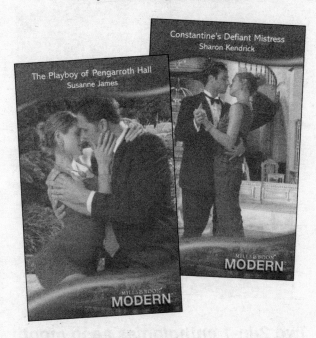

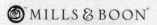